DEPENDENCE
to
INDEPENDENCE

I Think I Can ... I Know I Can

André J. Olivan Sr.

iUniverse, Inc.
Bloomington

Dependence to Independence
I Think I Can ... I Know I Can

iUniverse books may be ordered through booksellers or by contacting:

iUniverse
1663 Liberty Drive
Bloomington, IN 47403
www.iuniverse.com
1-800-Authors (1-800-288-4677)

ISBN: 978-1-4620-5501-2 (sc)
ISBN: 978-1-4620-5503-6 (e)
ISBN: 978-1-4620-5502-9 (dj)

Library of Congress Control Number: 2011960410

Printed in the United States of America

iUniverse rev. date: 11/18/2011

INTRODUCTION

Congratulations on taking your first step towards being accountable for your own independence. We wrote this book to help bridge the gap between what is traditionally taught to young people in our public school system and what is really needed in terms of skills in order to become an independent and self sufficient individual in our society.

Success can be defined many ways and real success encompasses many facets of life experiences. We hope that the skills taught in the book will give you the tools you need to be on your way to living a successful and satisfying life.

It is very exciting to be out on your own. You get to make the rules about how you spend your time and with whom. With each decision that you make there are consequences. Those consequences could be good or bad depending on the decision made. Many of life's lessons are learned through our life experiences. However, not all lessons need to be learned the hard way. It is our hope that some of the fundamental skills taught in this book will help you avoid costly and painful mistakes with uncomfortable and sometimes serious consequences.

Good luck on your independent journey. We hope you learn some basic skills from this book. We wish you all of life's success.

André J. Olivan

TABLE OF CONTENTS

Chapter One
Things To Consider

Your Quality of Life Depends 0n Your Choices

Evaluate Your Motive Behind Your Decision

Identify The Steps In Making A Good Decision

Identify The Difference Between Rationalization And Justification

Apply The Ben Franklin Technique

Confidence In Making A Good Decision

How to Make the Right Decision

Life is full of choices. There are always consequences resulting from the decisions you make. You are accountable for your own actions. It is therefore imperative that you try to make good choices and appropriate decisions. You have to establish a method or process to evaluate choices that have a direct affect on your future. In order to make a good and intelligent decision you must be honest with yourself. We want to help you keep the process simple.

There are many factors which go into how you make decisions. You are often influenced by emotions when making an important decision. This can be a disadvantage. You often make impulsive choices rather than being thoughtful in your decision making process. There are times when an immediate decision is completely appropriate. However most of the time it is in your best interest not to be too hasty when making the decision.

Impulse causes you to want something right now. Impulse is defined as "a sudden, unreasoned inclination to action". Rationalization can be thought of as talking yourself into something you want. It is convincing 'yourself' of something. It is best to avoid rationalizing your way into a decision. Needing is defined as "having an urgent or essential use for something lacking."

The first step in making a good decision is defining the difference between wants and needs. You will need to ask yourself questions to help you through the process of differentiating whether this is a want or a need decision. Ask yourself questions that will justify what you are trying to accomplish. Justifying is defined as, "searching for a reason, fact, circumstance, or explanation that will guide you to a solid and sound decision" for example, what is in your best interest over the long term.

To summarize, you should always be able to justify rather than rationalize your decisions.

Ben Franklin's Decision Making Process

Ben Franklin is one of the finest role models in our Country's history. He exemplified intelligence, integrity, confidence, and steadfast values. In his lifetime, he faced many personal obstacles and made both personal decisions as well as decisions on behalf of his country.

It has been said that Ben Franklin had one of the best and easiest ways of processing a decision. He simply took out a sheet of plain paper and drew a large T on it. On one side, he wrote the word pros and on one side the word cons. In his evaluation, he listed all the positive effects of the decision he was pondering under the pros side of the T. Under the cons side of the T, he listed all the negative effects of the proposed decision. Once he had listed all of his thoughts as either pros or cons, he simply chose the side with more items listed under it and made his decision accordingly.

To take this a step further, once you have completed the basic method used by Ben Franklin, you should go back and identify by order of importance each of the items listed in both pros and cons. One way to do this would be to identify each of the items listed in your pros and cons columns as either a Want; an Impulse; a Rationalization; a Need; or a Justification. By doing so, you can then weight the importance of each item and rather than simply making your decision based on the number of items in each category, you are now making your decision based on the importance or validity of each item in each category. Remember, it is very important that you be completely honest with yourself at this point.

Here are the steps -

1. List the advantages and disadvantages to the decision as outlined on the previous page

2. Grade each of the advantages and disadvantages using the following key.

3. Now, be honest with yourself and determine what is in your best interest when making a decision.

W	Wants	*To wish for, desire , or feel a need for something*
I	Impulse	*Sudden involuntary inclination, prompting action*
R	Rationalization	*Taking yourself into something, regardless of consequence*
N	Need	*Having an urgent use for something lacking*
J	Justification	*Searching for a reason, fact, circumstance, or explanation that will guide you to a solid and sound decision*

Once you have truthfully identified and graded each item by its importance or validity, the answer should then be very clear to you. The Needs and Justification items should have a greater weight on your decision than the Wants, Impulse, and Rationalization items. Instead of making an emotional decision, you have now made an appropriate and solid decision.

Occasionally, you will ponder an issue and still not be sure what the right decision should be. In a case such as this, go with your heart instinct. It is better to make some decision than to make no decision at all and get into the bad habit of procrastinating. Procrastination is putting things off. This causes undue stress and causes you not to be productive in your life.

To conclude, even a good decision can turn out to be a mistake. If you go through the process of being truthful in evaluating the best decision and it turns out to be a mistake, remember that the best learning curve often results from mistakes. More than likely, you won't repeat the mistake. None of us are perfect. Just try to consciously make good decisions. The rest will come with experience.

Personal Decision Making Example

Should I buy a new car?

	ADVANTAGES			DISADVANTAGES	
1.	I could drive a new car without worrying about it breaking down.	(J)	1.	Commitment to making $450 monthly payment for five years	(J)
2.	I would feel safer in a new car.	(W)	2.	The vehicle will depreciate rapidly.	(J)
3.	I really like the looks of that new model.	(J)	3.	Before the car is paid for, I will likely want a newer model.	(R)
4.	It really gets good gas mileage	(J)	4.	The insurance and registration will be more expensive than my current car.	(J)
5.	With a new pick-up truck, I could pull a boat.	(J)	5.	I don't own a boat and won't be able to afford one with my new truck payment.	(J)
6.	They approved my credit and my payment will only be $450 per month for sixty months.	(J)	6.	I don't have a garage to park my new car in so it stays nice.	(J)
7.	A New car is more environmentally friendly.	(J)	7.	I may not be able to buy a house if I have the car payment.	(J)
8.	The salesperson said that the car will be worth more than I owe on it in two years	(R)	8.	The model I like is one of the highest targeted vehicles for theft	(J)

9.	Buying a new car would reduce my repair/maintenance expenses.	(J)	9.	Our company is down-sizing and I could lose my job.		(J)
10.	A new car will last me much longer.	(J)	10.	The car payment is more than my rent.		(J)
	Total Justification	8		Total Justification		9

In this example, the disadvantages outweigh the advances 9 to 8 and therefore, the decision should be made NOT to purchase the car.

Sample Personal Decision Making Worksheet

What decision are you trying to make?

ADVANTAGES	DISADVANTAGES
1.	1.
2.	2.
3.	3.
4.	4.
5.	5.
6.	6.
7.	7.
8.	8.
9.	9.
10.	10.
Totals	Totals

Think carefully about the advantages and disadvantages of the decision. Be honest with yourself. Ask others for their input and advice and consider it objectively.

Chapter I Summary

1. Your quality of life depends on your choices:

- It's important for you to make good decisions

- Choices and decisions drive your actions

- You are accountable for your own actions

2. Motives that influence your decisions are:

- Wants

- Impulse

- Rationalization

- Needs

- Justification

3. You should identify your steps for making a good decision:

- Defining the difference between Wants and Needs

- Understanding and knowing the difference between - Rationalization and Justification

- Asking yourself justifying Questions

- Search for what is in your best interest over the long term

4. Identifying the difference between Rationalizing and Justifying reasons:

- Rationalization – A sudden unreasoned inclination to action. Also can be thought of as talking yourself into something you want.

- Justification – Searching for a reason, fact, circumstance, or explanation that will guide you to a solid and sound decision

5. Applying Decision Making techniques:

- Take a plain sheet of paper and draw a large T on it

- Label each side with advantages and disadvantages

- List any and all reasons for the decision you're about to make

- Label each reason as follows:

Wants	(W)
Impulse	(I)
Rationalization	(R)
Needs	(N)
Justification	(J)

- Eliminate all reasons other than needs and justifications

- Count number of items listed under advantages and disadvantages

- Your answer should be obvious

- Honesty will eliminate most emotional decisions

Chapter I Quiz

Is your quality of life really affected by your ability to make good sound decisions and why? Please explain your answer.

List the five categories used in the decision making evaluation worksheet.

Which two of the five is the most important? Why?

Which is the most detrimental to the process? Why?

Explain the importance of being honest with yourself as you go through the decision making process.

To summarize the process, is it best to justify or rationalize your decisions?

CHAPTER TWO
EMPLOYMENT

Prepare For Finding The Right Job

Creating The Image You Want

Where To Look For The Right Job

How To Present Yourself

Understanding The Interview

Interview Tips

Resume Development

Everyone should have a current resume prepared at all times. A resume is defined as a brief written account of personal, educational, and professional qualifications and experience. It is designed to assist a prospective employer in selecting from a number of candidates to fill a job vacancy. Many times, a resume will be requested before an interview is ever scheduled. It is therefore very important that the resume be impressive both in contents and in appearance.

There are a couple of things to keep in mind when developing your resume. First, the prospective employer is very busy. They are not interested in reading an entire book about you. They want to hit on the highlights – those characteristics which define you as being qualified for the position. Keep your resume short and to the point. Try to be precise in defining yourself. Don't use too many words. It is best to try to keep your resume down to a one page sheet if possible.

You can begin your resume by putting your name, address, and telephone number centered at the top of the page. You might want to enlarge or bold this information so that it stands out. If you have a fax number or e-mail address, you may want to include these as well. After this, you should included information using the following five points -

1. Objective - In this section of the resume, you will briefly define what your goals might be. For example, you might want to state that you seek a position working as a marketing representative utilizing your educational experience along with your interpersonal skills to contribute to the expansion of a growing company.

2. Skills and Qualifications - In this section, you should briefly state any special skills you possess and any special qualifications you have relating to the position you are applying for. For example you might have special computer knowledge and speak a second language fluently, or you may have other training or schooling.

3. Experience - Here you will list your prior employers starting with the most recent first and working your way backward.

You will state the period of time that you worked for that particular company along with their complete name and the mailing address. List the name of the title you held and a brief description of the duties or responsibilities involved. If there were promotions within one place of employment, be sure to mention them.

4. Education - This is where you list your formal educational background as well as special courses or training accomplishments. Like the Experience section, you begin by listing the most recent educational accomplishment first and work your way backwards. You need not include specific dates of educational accomplishments.

5. References - List the names and telephone numbers of individuals that a prospective employer can contact to ask for a recommendation about you. Examples of persons you might include as references are, prior supervisors, teachers, community leaders, coaches, or long time friends. Make sure these people know they have been listed as your references so that they can be prepared for any inquiries that they might receive. Many resumes simply state references available upon request. This is a way to keep the resume precise and protect your references from unnecessary calls. A serious prospective employer will request the list from you. You should then be prepared to provide them with a separate sheet of paper listing those references complete with telephone numbers. Three references should be adequate.

If you have never held a job before, you should state this fact under the "Experience" section. Simply write, "No prior employment history". You will want to emphasize your educational background and activities involvement such as community service, extra curricular activities involvement, club membership, volunteer work, sports participation, hobbies, and so on. Show the prospective employer how you have spent your time. If you have been going to school full time and have been involved in community service, this would explain not having had any gainful occupation thus far. There are also many books and software programs available which have been designed to customize and define a resume.

Sample Resume

Name
Address
City, State Zip
Telephone Phone
E-Mail Address

OBJECTIVE

Seeking a position in retail sales utilizing my interpersonal skills working with the general public in a fast paced, challenging environment with the possibility of advancement into management.

SKILLS AND QUALIFICATIONS

Experienced counter representative with knowledge of computerized cash register operation, accurate money handling, customer satisfaction issues involving complaints, inventory responsibilities, weekly ordering, and employee scheduling. I speak Spanish and English fluently.

EXPERIENCE

- 2008-2009 - Burgers R Us

Counter Representative – responsibilities included taking customer orders, customer complaints, ordering weekly supplies, handling cash, scheduling employees, doing weekly inventory.

EDUCATION

- 2007-2008 - Burgers R Us National School for Counter Sales Persons. Received first place in Burned Burger Complaint Specialist Competition

- 2003-2007 - ABC Joint Unified High School. Graduated with honors

REFERENCES

- Available upon Request

Where to Look for a Job

The first thing you need to consider when looking for a job is what you are qualified to do at this point in your life. You will also need to consider when you are available and what other commitments you have made for your time. Do you go to school or have children to consider? Think about how you will get to and from a job. Is there reliable transportation? This will help define where you should look for employment. Consider how much money you need to earn monthly in order to pay your expenses. Will there be any additional expenses from taking a specific job? For example, will you be required to purchase special attire or equipment? Will you need your own vehicle to perform your job? How much will it cost to get to and from work?

Once you have defined your needs and any limitations, you can begin searching for possible employment opportunities which match your availability, experience, and talents.

1. Newspaper - The classified advertisements section of any newspaper will have an entire section devoted to employment opportunities. Here you will find available jobs listed alphabetically, and by category. The Sunday paper typically has the largest classified section. Local newspapers are an excellent source of finding jobs offered in your area.

2. Employment Agencies - Employment agencies handle placement of qualified employees for employers. They interview and pre-qualify prior to sending a prospective candidate out to the employer. There are temporary agencies which specialize in temporary placement positions. Often, these temporary positions work into full time permanent positions. Some agencies charge the employee a fee, and some charge the employer a fee. Be sure to have clarification of this up front, especially if you are signing any kind of contract with them.

3. Employment Development Department (EDD) - The Employment Development Department has current lists of available jobs in your area. Many have web sites that you can visit and look for possible employment opportunities

4. Social Service Agencies - Most Social Services have job opportunity listings in their offices. Many have telephone hot lines where you hear a recorded list of current jobs available when you dial in. These lists are usually updated weekly. Check you local telephone directory for these numbers. Many social service agencies have career counselors who can send you to various job seminars, usually at little or no cost to you.

5. Bulletin Boards - You may be able to find job listings on bulletin boards on school campuses actual work facilities, local churches, or even at your local community centers.

6. Referrals - Don't forget that many opportunities for employment come simply from referrals or word of mouth. Get the word out there to the people you know that you are looking for specific job.

7. The World Wide Web - Today's internet offers unlimited access to employment opportunities. You can search for jobs, complete applications, and take pre-employment tests right on-line. Most employers have their own web-sites with employment opportunities listed. Many government entities have their employment information listed on-line as well.

The Interview Process

A job interview can be defined as a formal meeting in which one or more persons question, consult, or evaluate another person for the purposes of employment.

The key word noted above is FORMAL. A job interview is not a casual, familiar, friendly type of encounter. It is a formal event, meaning that the purpose of getting together is to conduct business and to see if there might be a match between you and the employer. The employer sets the pace in the interview. They are in charge. They will lead the meeting, not you. You are there under their guidelines. They have a specific need they are trying to address. You are being screened to see if you fit the bill. Many times, you will be in competition with other qualified applicants. It will be important that you set yourself apart from the other persons being interviewed.

It is critical that you arrive at your interview earlier than your scheduled appointment. Punctuality is one very important part of employment performance. You should never be late for an interview.

You need to come prepared for the interview with a copy of your resume, a pen, a notepad, and glasses if necessary. You should be appropriately dressed in conservative, clean and pressed attire. Shoes should match your clothing. Don't wear too much decorative jewelry or heavy perfume/cologne. Do not over apply make-up. Hair should be clean and styled. Your personal grooming will be an important part of their first impression of you.

Be attentive and try to act yourself. Remember, everyone goes through the same process as you. Try not to get nervous or anxious. Think about what the interviewer is asking of you and answer the questions in a clear and thoughtful manner, paying close attention to the questions. Don't get off the track and talk endlessly about something irrelevant to the question being asked. Do not interrupt the interviewer. Try to stay within a reasonable time frame when answering questions. And don't forget to maintain direct eye contact with your interviewer.

When the interview has been completed, be sure to thank the prospective employer/interviewer for taking the time to meet with you and be sure to express your availability and eagerness to accept the position. Ask them if they would like you to follow up with them in a few days. If not, ask them how you can learn whether you have been selected for the position.

Chapter Two - Summary

1. How to prepare yourself for finding the right job

   - Preparing your resume

   - Make sure you are qualified for the position for which you are applying

2. Where to look for the right job

   - Start with jobs that you are qualified for and which interest you

   - Temporary Placement Agencies

   - Local Newspaper Classified Advertisements

   - Personal referrals

   - Internet

   - Schools

3. First Impressions - Presenting yourself

   - Be punctual

   - Introduce yourself

   - Act confident not arrogant

   - Give a solid handshake

   - Give direct eye contact

   - Be courteous

   - Show good personal hygiene

   - Try to relax

4. Understanding the Interview Process

   - Review your qualifications

- Evaluate how you present yourself

- Judge your ability to respond to pressure

- Determine your personality and ability to work with others

- Allows you to ask questions about the job responsibilities

6. Do's and Don'ts of a Job Interview

- Do be punctual

- Do appear neat with good personal hygiene

- Don't wear sunglasses

- Don't chew gum

- Don't be inattentive

- Don't Interrupt

- Don't talk too much

Chapter Two Quiz

1. What is the most important tool for finding a job?

2. List four traits of projecting a good self imagine

3. List four tools for searching for a job

4. Define the job interview. During the interview process, describe what the employer's objectives are.

5. List two do's and two don'ts of the job interview

CHAPTER THREE
TRANSPORTATION

Automobiles - A Good Or Bad Investment

To Have A Car Payment Or Not To Have A Car Payment

Look, Shop, Compare, And Find The Best Buy

Pre-Purchase Inspection - A Must

The Best Deal

The Process Of Shopping And Negotiating

Final Details For The Purchase

Transportation - What do you need

Transportation is moving someone or something from one place to another. In metropolitan areas, there may not be such a need for transportation, at least for any distance. However, in more rural areas, one may need to travel many miles to simply get to work or to perform the simple task of shopping.

For many people, transportation seems to have become a symbol of status. Don't get too caught up in the notion that you are what you drive. Remember what you are trying to accomplish. You are trying to get from one place to another for a specific purpose.

The first thing that you need to determine when considering a mode of transportation is, what are your needs? The following are a few things to consider:

- Do you need a way to get to work?

- Do you need to transport something or someone?

- Where do you live?

- How much money do you have to spend?

Forms of Transportation

There are many forms of transportation. Depending on what part of the country you live in, you may have many options or only one. It is best to evaluate all of your options before you make any decision, especially a decision that will cost you money. The following is a list of different types of transportation.

- Walking

- Trains or Buses

- Subway or Ferry

- Car or Van Pools

- Individual automobile

- Bicycles

- Motorcycles or Scooters

- Trolley Cars or Airplanes

The cost associated with each of the means of transportation noted above will vary. If you live and work in a metropolitan area, a train, bus, ferry, or subway may be readily available to you at a fixed cost. On the other hand, walking or riding a bike may also be a viable means of getting where you need to go. In some cases, depending on your career, you may even need to commute via aircraft. At any rate, probably the most common means of transportation is the individual automobile. If, after evaluating your needs, you determine that an automobile is necessary, then there are many things you must know about owning a personal automobile. It is more costly than most think. Don't be fooled. Get the facts before you invest.

Cash or Finance

When deciding to purchase an individual personal automobile, probably the most important consideration is how much money do you have to spend on the vehicle. The answer to this question will make a huge difference on how you proceed. There are many different ways to go about buying a vehicle. You can either pay cash for it, meaning you pay the entire purchase price of the vehicle or you can purchase the vehicle using some system of financing. Financing is probably one of the most common ways to purchase a new vehicle. Basically, when you finance a vehicle, you are required to have some cash amount available for a down payment and a lender finances the balance of the purchase price involved. There are finance charges, or interest, added to the amount of money that you borrow or finance. The lender will require timely monthly payments on the loan for the specified period of the loan. In some cases, automobile loans can be stretched out over a period of years, often four or five years. For young people who do not have any established credit, they may need to have someone co-sign on the loan. This means that the co-signer accepts the financial responsibility if you should happen to default on the payments.

It is important to know whether or not you will be able to make the monthly payments. If you can not make those payments, the lender can come and repossess the vehicle. This means they can take it away from you, and impound it at a daily fee until you can make the payments. They can also auction off the vehicle and come after you and your co-signer for the difference in what it was sold for and your balance on the loan.

When considering financing as an option to purchase a vehicle, also remember that the vehicle depreciates as time goes by. Wear and tear, along with age, causes the vehicle to be worth less over time. During the first months of a financed vehicle, the loan balance will be greater than the value of the vehicle. This is not a good position to be in.

If possible, it is best to pay cash for a vehicle. By paying cash, you will only have the monthly costs of operation, maintenance, and insurance, rather than adding these costs on top of an auto loan payment. You should save enough money to purchase a reliable vehicle that will be dependable. You will then only need to budget the maintenance cost, gas cost, and the cost of insurance into your monthly budget.

It is very important to maintain the vehicle by keeping the oil and filter changed regularly per the user manual that came from the manufacturer of the vehicle. Check all other fluid levels frequently, including transmission, power steering, radiator coolant, and brake fluid. This will increase the life and dependability of your vehicle.

If possible, it is best not to finance a vehicle, especially if you are just getting started. The best thing you can do for yourself is start out with no car payment. At best, cars are a losing investment. Remember, for every day that you own the vehicle, it's value goes down. When you finance a car, you need to calculate the interest charges on top of the purchase price and remember that it won't actually be paid for, until three to five years have passed. Now, calculate the value of the vehicle..... and you can easily understand just what a losing proposition a financed car really is.

Choosing a Car

After you determine the amount of money you have to spend and make a decision on how to purchase the vehicle, you should now be ready to choose the type of vehicle to look for. Again, you need to evaluate your own specific usage requirements. The answers to these questions should all be Justifications rather than Rationalizations as we learned in Chapter One.

- How am I going to be using the car?

- Do I need 4-wheel drive?

- Do I need to haul anything?

- Am I transporting passengers or friends?

- How far will I be traveling?

- Will I use the freeways or mountain roads?

Where to Look and Shop

By asking yourself a few questions, you should be able to determine what type of vehicle you will be looking for. Based on the answers to the above questions, you should be able to determine whether you need, for example, a sport utility vehicle, commonly referred to as an SUV or an economical coupe or sedan.

Once you have an idea about the type of vehicle and the amount of money you have to spend, you can begin the actual search for a vehicle to fit your needs. There are many places to find vehicles that are for sale. Naturally, if you are looking for a new vehicle, there are many dealerships that would gladly sell you a car. You can even purchase a new vehicle over the internet. However, if you are in the market for a used vehicle, there are other places to search. The following are a few ideas about where to begin looking for a car:

- Newspaper classified advertisements

- Automobile Magazines

- New and Used Car lots

- The Internet

- Bulletin Boards

- Auction Yards

- For Sale signs posted in vehicles you may see around town

Finding the best buy involves doing your homework. Comparative shopping is the best way to know that you have gotten the most for your money. This is the best safeguard to insuring you don't buy out of impulse, but rather by completely researching your options.

Questions to Ask

Now that you have researched your options, you are ready to go take a look and test-drive some vehicles. There are two phases of inspecting and evaluating a prospective car. You will want to ask the owner several important questions about the automobile. You can do some of this over the phone when you call and make an appointment to come look at a car. Other questions are better addressed in person with the seller. Examples of questions you might want to ask over the phone to pre-qualify a vehicle would be:

- Confirm the year, make, and model of the vehicle advertised

- Confirm the price they are asking for the vehicle

- Ask for the mileage

- Are they the original owners? If not, how many previous owners and how long has this current owner had the vehicle?

- Why are they selling the vehicle?

- Describe the vehicle mechanically. Has it had any recent mechanical work?

- Does the current owner have all the service records or receipts for work performed on the vehicle?

- Has the vehicle been involved in any collision or had any bodywork done?

- How would you describe the interior and the paint?

If the above questions have been satisfactorily answered, make an appointment to go out and look at the car. It might be a good idea to take along a mature individual to act as a support person for you. Often times, people will try to take advantage of someone if they think they don't have good experience in purchasing or negotiating. Be sure to take along notes of the questions you asked in pre-qualifying the vehicle and confirm these things with the seller in person. Let the seller know that you have the notes and are serious.

The next step will be for you to visually inspect the vehicle. Make sure you examine it in the light where you can see all imperfections. The following is a list of items to look for:

Exterior

- Examine the paint

- Examine the body for dents

- Examine the chrome

- Look for any rust

- Check the windshield for any pits or cracks or scratches

- Examine the tires for wear – make sure you have at least 25% tread left on the tires or they should be replaced. You might want to negotiate this point if you decide to purchase the vehicle

Interior

- Examine the dash and gauges for cracks, holes, missing parts

- Examine the condition of the upholstery

- Examine the carpet

- Check to make sure the windows roll up and down

- Check to make sure the signals work

- Check to make sure the heater/air conditioner is operational

- Check to make sure the radio/tape player/compact disk player all work

- Check to make sure the windshield wipers are in good condition and that they work

- Check to make sure that all seatbelts are in good working condition

When inspecting the engine area, you will want to open the hood and inspect it first before starting the engine and then again with the engine running. A flashlight will help you with this visual inspection

- Check for any oil leaks

- Check all fluid levels and color

- Check the radiator for any rust

- Check the battery for corrosion

- Check all electrical wiring for any wear

- Check all hoses for cracks or holes

- Check to make sure the engine does not smell burnt

- Listen for any clanking, squeaking, skipping, or missing sounds

- Make certain all fluid caps are in place

If after you have visually inspected the exterior, interior, and engine areas, and you are satisfied with what you have seen so far, the next step would be to take the vehicle for a test drive.

When test driving a vehicle, you should not turn the radio on. This way, you will be able to listen to the engine as you drive at various speeds. If you can't hear the engine, you may not be aware of any sounds that could signal mechanical problems. Be sure to take the vehicle onto the freeway so that you can accelerate to see how much power it has. You will want to go up hills, down hills, and around curves in order to see how it steers, brakes, and accelerates. You should check the gauges during the test drive to make sure there are no problems such as overheating from lack of oil or coolants.

Pre-Purchase Inspection

If you are satisfied with your inspection and test drive and are considering negotiating to purchase the vehicle, you might want to consider taking it to a licensed mechanic for a pre-purchase inspection. The average cost to you would be one or two hours labor charge by the mechanic. This could be money well spent if you are uncertain about the mechanical soundness of the vehicle. The trained mechanic will do an overview of the vehicle as well as a compression test and will check the coolant system under pressure. They will also check the brakes, which is an extremely important safety issue.

If the vehicle checks out to your satisfaction and you decide you want to purchase it, you will want to review any faults you have noted and use these points to negotiate a fair price with the seller. Remember that the asking price may be negotiable. It is always best to get a good buy. As a starting point, you could offer 20% below the asking price. This can be intimidating to the first time buyer. Again, it can be helpful to take along someone with some experience to assist you in this regard.

Smog Certification

In some states, the DMV will require that the vehicle pass a smog test. It is your responsibility to take the vehicle to a licensed smog shop and have them perform the smog test. If the vehicle does not pass the smog test, you will be required to make any necessary repairs in order to get it to pass the smog test before you will be able to register it. This can be costly and should certainly be addressed with the seller prior to the final purchase of the vehicles. Smog certificates are electronically transmitted to the DMV by the smog shop.

The Purchase Process

Once you arrive at an agreed price between yourself and the seller, along with paying the seller the money for the vehicle, you will need to write out a purchase agreement. This agreement should state the date, purchase price of the vehicle, description of the vehicle (license number and VIN number), and names of the buyer and the seller. Both parties need to sign the purchase agreement. There should also be a statement reference releasing the seller of their liability upon the purchase of the vehicle (available on line or at the DMV). The seller will also need to sign the Pink Slip which is the legal title to the vehicle. You will need both of these important documents before you leave with your new automobile at the time of purchase.

Finalizing the Purchase - Transfer of Title and Registration

The next thing you need to take care of is the transfer of title and registration on the vehicle. This should be taken care of right away. You will need to take the title, the purchase agreement, and the Release of Liability Form to the Department of Motor Vehicles. In many states, you will also need to show the DMV agent your proof of Insurance. Your insurance agent can usually provide you this documentation if you call beforehand and give them the vehicle identification number (VIN) number of the car you are buying. At that time, you will also be required to pay sales tax based on the purchase price of the vehicle. The DMV will assist you in completing the paper work to transfer the title into your name. They will take the pink slip. You will receive the title back by mail after they have processed the change in ownership. You will be required to pay registration and title transfer fees at this time.

Insurance

Insurance is defined as the business of insuring property, life, or persons against loss or harm arising in specified contingencies, in return for payments. It is basically the transfer of risk from you to an insurance company in exchange for premium, or money. Insurance is a contract of coverage in which one party agrees to indemnify or reimburse another for loss that occurs under the terms of the contract.

A vehicle is a liability. This means it can cause damage to others. This includes damage to someone else's property or to another person. A moving vehicle is a 3,000 pound traveling object, which upon impact can cause serious damage and/or injury If it causes damage and/or injuries to someone other than yourself, you as the owner are liable for those damages and/or injuries. This is where the need to insure your vehicle comes in. It is required by all states that you have proper liability coverage for your vehicle or in some states, you may have the option to post a bond instead.

There are several different types of insurance coverage to consider for your vehicle. The first is Liability coverage. As mentioned earlier, if something is damaged or someone is hurt as a result of the operation of your vehicle, you as the owner become liable for those damages. Liability insurance coverage pays damages to others on your behalf. There are various limits of liability coverage available. Consult with a licensed insurance agent or broker as to which limits are appropriate for you.

Uninsured or Underinsured Motorist is another insurance coverage type. This type of insurance pays you and your passengers if an uninsured or underinsured vehicle strikes you. Approximately 25% of the vehicles on the road today do not carry insurance coverage. If you are unfortunate enough to be hit by one of those vehicles, you will need uninsured or underinsured motorist coverage. Again, consult with a licensed insurance agent or broker.

Comprehensive and collision coverage pay for physical damages to your vehicle. Collision coverage pays for damage to the vehicle as a result of collision with any other objects. Comprehensive coverage is damage to the vehicle when caused by something other than collision, such as: falling trees, hail, flood, etc. When considering whether to insure your vehicle for comprehensive and collision coverage, you will want to evaluate the value of your vehicle in comparison to the premium charges associated with this type of coverage. Again, a licensed insurance agent or broker will be able to assist you in making this decision

It is critical that you have proper insurance coverage for your vehicle. There is a wide range of coverage and limits available. Pricing also varies. When you are in the market for insurance coverage, make sure you have a licensed agent or broker to explain the coverage options completely and be sure to do some price comparing. You want adequate coverage for a reasonable price.

In conclusion, purchasing a vehicle is a major step. Remember that there are literally millions of automobiles out there. Don't be in a hurry. Do your homework; make sure you do some comparative shopping. Look at lots of cars! The best you can do is purchase a vehicle at below wholesale price and pay cash for it.

André J. Olivan Sr.

Automobile Safety Checklist

Automobile Safety Checklist

Refer to the appropriate service manual, owner's manual, and service bulletin(s) for fluid levels, specifications, and procedures. Draw a line through any item that does not apply.

Under Vehicle

- ☐ Check for leaks: engine, transmission, differential, transfer case, cooling system, brakes, steering, fuel and exhaust
- ☐ Transmission oil (M/T only)
- ☐ Transfer case oil
- ☐ Front and/or rear differential oil
- ☐ Shift-on-the-fly system oil
- ☐ Parking brake cables
- ☐ Visually check the entire undercarriage for damage and loose or missing parts
- ☐ Install frame hole plugs

Under Hood

- ☐ Battery charged
- ☐ Fuses installed
- ☐ Engine oil
- ☐ Automatic transmission fluid
- ☐ Coolant level and concentration (50/50 solution of antifreeze and water)
- ☐ Brake fluid
- ☐ Power steering fluid
- ☐ Windshield washer fluid
- ☐ A/C belt tension
- ☐ Alternator belt tension
- ☐ Hose clamps
- ☐ Clutch pedal free play (at pedal)
- ☐ P/S belt tension

Exterior

- ☐ Tire pressure
- ☐ Wheel nut torque
- ☐ All exterior lights
- ☐ Headlight aim
- ☐ Keys, locks operation
- ☐ Remote access key operation
- ☐ License plate bracket

- ☐ Install spare tire cover, check spare tire mounting and tire pressure

Trunk

- ☐ Rear seat release from inside the trunk
- ☐ Trunk light
- ☐ Sun/moonroof tools
- ☐ Tire tools and jack
- ☐ Spare tire pressure

Interior

- ☐ Fuses installed
- ☐ Brake pedal free play (at pedal)
- ☐ Parking brake adjustment
- ☐ Interior lights
- ☐ Ignition warning beeper
- ☐ Turn the ignition ON, and check all indicator lights, beepers, and chimes
- ☐ Immobilizer indicator
- ☐ Door open indicator
- ☐ Trunk open indicator
- ☐ High beam flasher
- ☐ High beam indicator
- ☐ Instrument lights
- ☐ Turn signal/hazard lights
- ☐ Engine starts only in P or N
- ☐ A/T shift lock release
- ☐ Starter interlock (M/T only)
- ☐ Shift interlock (A/T only)
- ☐ Horn
- ☐ Clear HomeLink transmitter
- ☐ Clock (set to correct time)
- ☐ Rear window defogger
- ☐ Manual/power door locks
- ☐ Sun/moonroof, sunshade
- ☐ Manual/power windows
- ☐ Manual/power mirrors
- ☐ Mirror defogger

- ☐ Tilt steering wheel
- ☐ Audio system and security code card
- ☐ Beverage holder
- ☐ Cargo area cover/cargo net
- ☐ Manual/power seat adjustments
- ☐ Head restraints
- ☐ Folding rear seat
- ☐ Folding table
- ☐ Childproof locks
- ☐ Glove/security compartments
- ☐ Fuel filler door release and fuel cap
- ☐ Hood release
- ☐ Trunk release
- ☐ Electric tailgate glass release
- ☐ Cigarette lighter
- ☐ Accessory power socket
- ☐ Owner's/Warranty manuals, tire warranty information booklet, and any applicable hang tags
- ☐ Jack, handle, and lug wrench mounting

Accessories

- ☐ Installation
- ☐ Operation

Road Test

- ☐ Cold start
- ☐ Speedometer/odometer/trip meter
- ☐ Tachometer operation
- ☐ Check all gauges (fuel, temp, voltage, oil)
- ☐ Braking performance (normal and ABS)
- ☐ Clutch operation
- ☐ Shift smoothness/ease
- ☐ Upshift indicator
- ☐ Shifting in and out of 4WD

- ☐ Shifting to and from 4L
- ☐ Driveability
- ☐ Engine performance
- ☐ Cruise control operation
- ☐ Turn signal canceling
- ☐ Power steering performance
- ☐ Steering wheel centered and free from vibration (tire balance)
- ☐ Tracks straight
- ☐ Heat/defrost/vent controls
- ☐ Window washer aim (front and rear)
- ☐ Front/rear wipers
- ☐ A/C controls and operation
- ☐ Radiator and condenser fans on with A/C on
- ☐ Idle speed with A/C on and off
- ☐ Parking brake operation
- ☐ No squeaks or rattles

Detail

- ☐ Protective plastic removed from interior
- ☐ Protective covering removed from exterior

Cleanliness

- ☐ Interior
- ☐ Exterior

General Fit and Finish

- ☐ Interior
- ☐ Exterior
- ☐ Doors, hood, trunk, and tailgate opening/closing quality
- ☐ Paint free from environmental fallout
- ☐ No scratches or dents

Chapter Three - Summary

1. Cars are a poor investment

   - They depreciate daily

   - Maintenance is costly

   - Cost of operation is rising

2. Without a car payment, you still have the following expenses:

   - Registration & License

   - Insurance

   - Operational Cost

   - Depreciation

3. By financing a vehicle, the following expenses are in addition to those noted above

   - Monthly loan amount

   - Monthly interest charges

4. Finding the best buy includes three major actions

   - Look – there are always great deals

   - Shop -using several resources

   - Compare – quality and pricing

5. Pre-Purchase Inspection

   - Know the car before you buy it

   - Look for tell-tale signs

   - Listen for warning signs

   - Take it for a test drive

   - Final inspection by a professional mechanic

6. The Best Deal

- Finding an exceptionally clean car

- Finding one that has low mileage

- Doing your homework

- Buying it at or below wholesale price

7. Shopping and Negotiating

- Negotiate

- Look for pricing weaknesses

- Start below asking price because you can always go up

8. Final Details for your purchase should include

- Make sure the vehicle will pass smog certification

- Transfer of title and registration

- Review safety check sheet

- Make sure you have proper insurance coverage before taking possession of any vehicle

Chapter Three - Quiz

1. Are cars a good investment and if so, why?

2. What expenses do you have when you own a car both?

3. List the three major actions for find the best buy.

4. List three reasons for the Pre-Purchase inspection.

5. What are the three main components for the Best Deal?

6. What is the one thing should you never do when negotiating?

CHAPTER FOUR
GETTING YOUR OWN PLACE

Dependence To Independence - Where To Start

Selecting The Right Place

Biggest Consideration: Location, Location, Location

Taking Action - Setting Yourself Up

Best Type Of Agreements

Roommate Agreements

Getting Your Own Place

So, you're thinking about getting your own place. This is probably one of the most exciting decisions you'll make. Finding just the right place is really fun and exciting. Up to this point in your life, you may have been dependent on someone else for your housing arrangements. Most of us don't appreciate how wonderful this type of arrangement is until you are on your own financially, or supporting other people. But, there comes that time in everyone's life when you no longer want to conform to someone else's rules and standards, so you decide to go out on your own and live by your own rules in your own house. You make that decision to become completely independent and fully self-sufficient. The first thing you need to do is evaluate what your preferences might be.

- Do you want to live alone?

- Do you want roommates?

- Can you afford the expense by yourself or do you need to share the expense with others like you?

- Do you want to rent on a monthly basis or do you want to lock into a place for a period of time?

- Where do you want to live?

- Do you have children to consider?

- Do you have pets?

Depending on what you determine from the considerations listed above, there are different arrangements to evaluate. For instance, you may want to live alone, in which case you would be completely responsible for all aspects of maintaining your housing. You would not need to consider someone else's housekeeping standards or living habits. You would also not be relying on anyone else's financial contribution to maintain the roof over your head. For some individuals, this would be their preference. They may enjoy the quiet undisturbed environment that living alone affords.

Roommates - Sharing Rental Housing

If you don't want to live alone, you may want to consider finding a roommate in a shared rental arrangement. Roommates are often friends or people we know from somewhere, but sometimes, you may find a roommate through an ad in the newspaper or through a rental agency. College campuses often have lists of individuals looking to share a rental with one or more persons. Whether your roommate happens to be a friend, a co-worker, or a perfect stranger, you need to keep in mind that a shared rental arrangement is a business arrangement. If it isn't handled properly, friendships can be lost and financial troubles can arise.

There are Many Types of Housing

Studio Apartment – A small place that typically combines the living room, bedroom, and kitchenette into one room. Usually, the studio apartment is less expensive than a one bedroom apartment. This type of housing would best suit an individual resident.

Apartment / Condominium – A multiple unit building. Each unit may have one or more bedrooms, a separate living room, kitchen, dining room, and bathroom. Some even have their own laundry hook-ups in the unit itself or they may have a laundry facility with coin operated machines. Some have private patios or balconies and fireplaces. There are really a wide range of amenities when looking into apartments and condominiums. The grounds are cared for by the management of the facility. They often have a common recreation area with swimming pool, weight room, tennis courts, basketball courts, and saunas. Some are really quite fancy. Others are very basic.

Duplex – Two single family residences connected by one common wall. Usually, each separate residence has its own separate yard and garage.

Single Family Dwelling – Standard house with lots of different layouts and options. This type of housing best suits a family or a shared rental arrangement. Each tenant has their own bedroom and shares the common areas.

Location, Location, Location

Location is probably the biggest consideration in beginning the search for your own place. What area do you want to live in and for what reason? It may be that you need to live near your work or school. On the other hand, you may desire to live in a neighborhood because of the amenities. It may also afford an easy commute to work or school.

There are many resources available when looking for a place to rent. The following are some common places to look:

- Classified advertisement section of the local newspaper

- Rental magazines

- Local Real Estate offices

- The Internet

- Local college bulletin boards or school papers

- Neighborhood churches

- Local Chamber of Commerce

- For Rent signs posted at rental properties

- Network with the people you know. Often rental arrangements are made simply through word of mouth

Moving can be quite costly. It is best not to move around too often because of this fact. It also looks better on rental applications, job applications, credit applications, etc. when you have lived in one place for a good period of time rather than moving around frequently. It gives a more stable impression. For these reasons, you will want to be careful when considering where to live. Don't rush into the first place you look at. Do some comparison shopping and carefully consider how the place suits your specific needs. Some things to consider when evaluating a place to live might be:

- Is the neighborhood safe?

- Is the location convenient for me?

- Are the amenities appropriate for me?

- Is the place the right size to suit my needs?

- Is parking available?

- Is it quiet enough for me? Is there enough recreation?

- Is there accessible public transportation if I need it?

- Is the building in good condition?

- Is there convenient shopping, health care facilities, etc?

- Is it affordable for me?

- What is required to get into the place?

The Application Process

After researching the market, you've found something you like and want to rent. The first step, after looking at the place, would be to express your interest. The landlord will require that you complete an application if you wish to rent their property. The application will be signed and dated and will include information such as personal data, occupational information, and references. This information will be evaluated. The prospective landlord may also do a background check, including a credit check and reference inquiry. This is to verify that the information you have provided on your application is accurate and true. Most landlords are looking to rent to tenants who demonstrate stability in occupation. If your application is approved, the next step will be to satisfy the financial requirement and sign the rental or lease agreement. It is common for a landlord to require the first month's rent along with the last month's rent and a security or cleaning deposit to be paid at the time the agreement is signed.

It is best to do a walk through with the landlord prior to renting the facility. Refer to the Move In/Move Out Form at the end of this section for examples of areas that should be noted prior to moving anything into the facility. You will go through each room and check the pre-existing condition. Any discrepancy should be noted and the form signed by both the tenant(s) and the landlord and/or property manager. This will aid in protecting both the landlord and the tenant against later disputes pertaining to any pre-existing damage versus damages which may happen while you inhabited the premises.

The next step is to sign the lease or rental agreement. They are lease agreements and month-to-month agreements. The basic difference between these contracts is the length of time that you and the landlord agree upon for you to occupy the property. In a lease contract, there is a specific time defined in the contract, for instance, one year. The tenant is obligated to pay the monthly fee for the entire lease time specified even if circumstances change and you move out early. With a month to month contract, either party can give the other notice to vacate with only a one month's notice to the other party. This is one of the major considerations in signing a rental agreement.

It is critical that you read the entire lease contract and fully understand it prior to signing. Since it is considered a binding contract, it might be advisable to seek legal advice prior to entering into the contract.

You should be prepared to pay an amount of up to three months rent when signing the rental or lease contract. Remember that the landlord collects the rent in advance. They do not want to have to chase tenants down to collect rent due. They also want to have their property returned to them in the same condition in which it was leased or rented out. For this reason, they may collect a security and/or cleaning deposit. If repairs or additional cleaning is required after you vacate the facility, the deposit can be retained by the landlord to cover such expenses.

If you are going into a rental with roommates, it might be a good idea to put the agreed terms into writing and have each roommate sign it. As we mentioned earlier in this section, entering into a rental contract with roommates is a business relationship regardless if the roommates are best friends. It is best to have a clear understanding of what is required of each person before signing any rental contract with a landlord. The following might be items to include in your contract:

- When are monies due? How are expenses to be divided between the parties.

- What agreements are made between the parties as respects maintenance of the common areas?

- Privacy

- Behavior expectations

- Consequences for illegal activities

Please refer to the example Roommate/Shared Rental Agreement form at the end of this section for what might be included in such an agreement.

Setting up Utilities and Services

In some cases, the rent you pay for a property may include some utilities such as trash, water, and/or cable/telephone/internet service. In other cases, the rent you pay only covers the unit itself and does not include any utility services. In this case, you will need to consider what utilities you want or need and set up an account in your name. If you've never had an account with your local electric or gas company, they may require a security deposit before initiating service to you for the first time. Generally, after one year of service, they will refund the deposit to you. You can find the telephone numbers to utility companies listed in your local telephone directory. A simple phone call is the first step in setting up these services.

Some services can be initiated by computer. In other cases, a technician will actually need to come to the address and activate the service for you. In this case, there is generally a fee and someone will need to be at the premises to meet the technician and to sign the work order.

Again, if you are entering into a rental agreement with roommates, you will need to make sure everyone is in agreement about what services you are ordering and how those services are going to be set up and paid for. Remember that the person whose name appears on the bill is responsible for the payment of those services. Make sure everyone is on the same page about this. It will save you much grief later on. If it's not spelled out, each roommate can be held responsible for the standards and the financial obligations of the other roommates.

Rental Application

RENTAL APPLICATION

PERSONAL DATA

Name	Date of Birth	Social Security No		
		Drivers Lic No	Expir Date	
Name of Co-Tenant		Social Security No		
Present Address		Drivers Lic No	Expir. Date	
City-State/Zip	Res Phone	Bus. Phone		
How long at present address	Landlord or Agent	Phone		
Previous Address	How long	Landlord or Agent	Phone	
City State-Zip				
Occupants { Relationships / Ages		Pets?		
Car Make	Year	Model	Color	License No.

OCCUPATION

	PRESENT OCCUPATION*	PRIOR OCCUPATION*	CO-TENANT S OCCUPATION
Occupation			
Employer			
Self-employed, doing business as			
Business Address			
Business Phone			
Type of Business			
Position held			
Name and Title of Supervisor			
How long			
Monthly Gross Income			

*If employed or self-employed less than two years give same information on prior occupation

REFERENCES

Bank Reference		Address		Phone	
CREDIT REFERENCE	ACCOUNT NO	ADDRESS	HIGHEST AMOUNT OWED	PURPOSE OF CREDIT	ACCOUNT OPEN OR DATE CLOSED

PERSONAL REFERENCE	ADDRESS	PHONE	LENGTH OF ACQUAINTANCE	OCCUPATION

NEAREST RELATIVE	ADDRESS	PHONE	CITY	RELATIONSHIP

Have you ever filed a petition for bankruptcy? _____ Have you ever been evicted from any tenancy? _____

Have you ever willfully and intentionally refused to pay any rent when due? _____

I DECLARE THAT THE FOREGOING INFORMATION IS TRUE AND CORRECT, AUTHORIZE ITS VERIFICATION AND THE OBTAINING OF CONSUMER CREDIT REPORT

I agree that Landlord may terminate any agreement entered into in reliance on any misstatement made above   DATED _____

Applicant _____   Applicant _____

The Professional Education Institute   PEI 13

51

André J. Olivan Sr.

Move in/Move out Form

MOVE IN/MOVE OUT FORM

Resident's Name: _____   Move-In: _____

Property Address: _____   Move-Out: _____

MASTER BEDROOM

Walls/Ceiling	
Floors	
Windows	
Screens	
Window Covering	
Light Fixture	

BEDROOM

Walls/Ceiling	
Floors	
Windows	
Screens	
Window Covering	
Light Fixture	

BEDROOM

Walls/Ceiling	
Floors	
Windows	
Screens	
Window Covering	
Light Fixture	

BEDROOM

Walls/Ceiling	
Floors	
Windows	
Screens	
Window Covering	
Light Fixture	

BATHROOM

Walls/Ceiling	
Floors	
Light Fixture	
Sink	
Toilet	
Tub Shower	
Medicine Cabinet	
Window	
Window Covering	
Exhaust Fan	
Towel Racks	

BATHROOM

Walls/Ceiling	
Floors	
Light Fixture	
Sink	
Toilet	
Tub Shower	
Medicine Cabinet	
Window	
Window Covering	
Exhaust Fan	
Towel Racks	

OTHER _____

LIVING ROOM

Walls/Ceiling
Floors
Light Fixture
Windows
Window Covering
Screens
Fire Place

DINING ROOM AREA

Walls/Ceiling
Floors
Light Fixture
Windows
Screens
Window Covering

KITCHEN

Walls/Ceiling
Floors
Windows
Screens
Window Covering
Light Fixture
Sink
Cabinets
Range & Oven
Refrigerator
Dishwasher
Garbage Disposal

SERVICE EQUIPMENT

Air Conditioner
Heater

UTILITY AREA

Floors
Walls/Ceiling
Washer/Dryer

GARAGE/STORAGE

Floors
Walls/Ceilings
Light Fixture
Windows
Screens

EXTERIOR

Walls
Trim

LAWN LANDSCAPE

MISCELLANEOUS

Door Opener
Keys

The undersigned acknowledges that the above is the condition of the Property on moving in.

Resident: _____

Resident: _____

Management: _____

The undersigned acknowledges that the above is the condition of the Property on vacating the premises.

Resident: _____

Resident: _____

Management: _____

André J. Olivan Sr.

Residential Lease Agreement

RESIDENTIAL LEASE/RENTAL AGREEMENT

This agreement made this _____ day of _____, 19 _____, is between _____ (hereinafter called Management) and _____ (hereinafter called Resident). Management leases to Resident, and Resident rents from Management, residential unit located at _____ under the following conditions:

TERM: 1. The initial term of this lease shall be _____ beginning _____ 19 _____ and ending Noon _____ 19 _____.

POSSESSION: 2. If there is a delay in delivery of possession by Management, rent shall be abated on a daily basis until possession is granted. If possession is not granted within seven (7) days after the beginning day of initial term, then Resident may void this agreement and have full refund of any deposit. Management shall not be liable for damages for delay in possession.

RENT: 3. Rent is payable monthly, in advance, at a rate of _____ dollars ($ _____) per month, during the term of this agreement on the first day of each month at the office of Management or at such other place Management may designate. Tenant agrees to pay $20 for each dishonored check.

RENT DISCOUNT: 4. Time is of the essence of this agreement. If the rent is accepted before the close of the business day, on the 4th of each month, the rate will be _____ dollars ($ _____), any returned check will be considered as unpaid rent and not subject to discount.

EVICTION: 5. If the rent called for in paragraph 3 hereof has not been paid by the fifteenth (15th) of the month, then Management shall automatically and immediately have the right to take out a Dispossessory Warrant and have Resident, his family and possessions, evicted from the premises.

INDEMNIFICATION DEPOSIT: 6. Management acknowledges receipt of _____ dollars ($ _____), as a deposit to indemnify owner against damage to the property and for Resident's fulfillment of the conditions of this agreement. Deposit will be returned to Resident less a $50 carpet cleaning charge, thirty days after residence is vacated if:

    (a) Lease term has expired or agreement has been terminated by both parties; and

    (b) All monies due Management by Resident have been paid; and

    (c) Residence is not damaged and is left in its original condition, normal wear and tear excepted; and

    (d) Management is in receipt of copy of paid final bills on all utilities (includes gas, electric, water, garbage, and telephone).

    (e) Deposit will not be returned if Resident leaves before lease time is completed. Deposit may be applied by Management to satisfy all or part of Resident's obligations and such act shall not prevent Management from claiming damages in excess of the deposit. Resident may not apply the deposit to any of the rent payment.

    (f) Keys have been returned and a forwarding address left. Resident acknowledges that he has approved and signed the "Residential Rental Property Move in. Move Out Inspection Form" for any existing damages to residence and has been given the right to inspect same.

RENEWAL TERM: 7. It is the intent of both parties that this lease is for a period of _____ months and that the last month's rent will apply only to the last month of the lease period. Should this lease be breached by the Resident, both the last month's rent and the indemnification deposit shall be forfeited as liquidated damages and the Resident will owe rent through the last day of occupancy.

EARLY TERMINATION: 8. Resident may terminate this agreement before expiration of the original term by:

    (a) Giving Management at least one month's written notice to be effective only on the last day of a given month; plus

    (b) Paying all monies due through date of termination, plus

    (c) Paying an amount equal to one month's rent; plus

    (d) Returning residence in a clean, ready-to-rent condition.

    (e) Resident must pay for advertising necessary to rent residence

SUBLET: 9. Resident may not sublet residence or assign this lease without written consent of Management.

CREDIT APPLICATION: 10. Management having received and reviewed a credit application filled out by Resident, and Management having relied upon the representations and statements made therein as being true and correct, has agreed to enter into this rental agreement with Resident. Resident and Management agree the credit application the Resident filled out when making application to rent said residence is hereby incorporated by reference and made a part of this rental agreement. Resident further agrees if he has falsified any statement on said application, Management has the right to terminate rental agreement immediately, and further agrees Management shall be entitled to keep any security deposit and any prepaid rent as liquidated damages. Resident further agrees in the event Management exercises its option to terminate rental agreement, Resident will remove himself, his family, and possessions from the premises within 24 hours of notification by Management of the termination of this lease. Resident further agrees to indemnify Management for any damages to property of Management including, but not limited to, the cost of making residence suitable for renting to another Resident, and waives any right of "set-off" for the security deposit and prepaid rent which was forfeited as liquidated damages.

FIRE AND CASUALTY: 11. If residence becomes uninhabitable by reason of fire, explosion, or by other casualty, Management may, at its option, terminate rental agreement or repair damages within 30 days. If Management does not do repairs within this time or if building is fully destroyed, the rental agreement hereby created is terminated. If Management elects to repair damages, rent shall be abated and prorated from the date of the fire, explosion, or other casualty to the date of reoccupancy, providing during repairs Resident has vacated and removed Resident's possessions as required by Management. The date of reoccupancy shall be the date of notice that residence is ready for occupancy.

HOLD OVER: 12. Resident shall deliver possession of residence in good order and repair to Management upon termination or expiration of this agreement.

RIGHT OF ACCESS: 13. Management shall have the right of access to residence for inspection and repair or maintenance during reasonable hours. In case of emergency, Management may enter at any time to protect life and prevent damage to the property.

USE: 14. Residence shall be used for residential purposes only and shall be occupied only by the persons named in Resident's application to lease. The presence of an individual residing on the premises who is not a signator on the rental agreement will be sufficient grounds for termination of this agreement. Residence shall be used so as to comply with all state, county, and municipal laws and ordinances. Resident shall not use residence or permit it to be used for any disorderly or unlawful purpose or in any manner so as to interfere with other Residents' quiet enjoyment of their residence.

54

PROPERTY LOSS:

15. Management shall not be liable for damage to Resident's property of any type for any reason or cause whatsoever, except where such is due to Management's gross negligence. Resident acknowledges that he is aware that he is responsible for obtaining any desired insurance for fire, theft, liability, etc., on personal possessions, family, and guests.

PETS:

16. Animals, birds, or pets of any kind shall not be permitted inside the residential unit at any time unless the prior written approval of Management has been obtained.

INDEMNIFICATION:

17. Resident releases Management from liability for and agrees to indemnify Management against losses incurred by Management as a result of (a) Resident's failure to fulfill any condition of this agreement; (b) any damage or injury happening in or about residence or premises to Resident's invitees or licensees or such person's property; (c) Resident's failure to comply with any requirements imposed by any governmental authority; and (d) any judgement, lien, or other encumbrance filed against residence as a result of Resident's action.

FAILURE OF MANAGEMENT TO ACT:

18. Failure of Management to insist upon compliance with the terms of this agreement shall not constitute a waiver of any violation.

REMEDIES CUMULATIVE:

19. All remedies under this agreement or by law or equity shall be cumulative. If a suit for any breach of this agreement establishes a breach by Resident, Resident shall pay to Management all expenses incurred in connection therewith.

NOTICES:

20. Any notice required by this agreement shall be in writing and shall be delivered personally or mailed by registered or certified mail.

REPAIRS:

21. Management will make necessary repairs to the exterior with reasonable promptness *after receipt of written notice* from Resident. Resident shall make all necessary repairs to interior and keep premises in a safe, clean, and sanitary condition. Resident shall make contact with all repair or service people and will be responsible for paying the first $25 of any charge. Resident may not remodel or paint or structurally change, nor remove any fixture therefrom without written permission from Management.

ABANDONMENT:

22. If Resident removes or attempts to remove property from the premises other than in the usual course of continuing occupancy, without having first paid Management all monies due, residence may be considered abandoned, and Management shall have the right without notice, to store or dispose of any property left on the premises by Resident. Management shall also have the right to store or dispose of any of Resident's property remaining on the premises after the termination of this agreement. Any such property shall be considered Management's property and title thereto shall vest in Management.

MORTGAGEE'S RIGHTS:

23. Resident's rights under this lease shall at all times be automatically junior and subject to any deed to secure debt which is now or shall hereafter be placed on premises of which residence is part; if requested, Resident shall execute promptly any certificate that Management may request to specifically implement the subordination of this paragraph.

RULES AND REGULATIONS:

24. (a) Signs: Resident shall not display any signs, exterior lights, or markings. No awnings or other projections shall be attached to the outside of the building.

(b) Locks: Resident is prohibited from adding locks to, changing, or in any way altering locks installed on the doors. All keys must be returned to Management of the premises upon termination of the occupancy.

(c) Entrances, walks, lawns, and driveways shall not be obstructed or used for any purpose other than ingress and egress.

(d) Radio or television aerials shall not be placed or erected on the roof or exterior.

(e) Parking: Non-operative vehicles are not permitted on premises. Any such non-operative vehicle may be removed by Management at the expense of Resident owning same, for storage or public or private sale, at Management's option, and Resident owning same shall have no right of recourse against Management therefor.

(f) Storage: No goods or materials of any kind or description which are combustible or would increase fire risk or shall in any way increase the fire insurance rate with respect to the premises or any law or regulation, may be taken or placed in a storage area or the residence itself. Storage in all such areas shall be at Resident's risk and Management shall not be responsible for any loss or damage.

(g) Walls: No nails, screws or adhesive hangers except standard picture hooks, shade brackets, and curtain rod brackets may be placed in walls, woodwork, or any part of residence.

(h) Guest: Resident shall be responsible and liable for the conduct of his guests. Act of guests in violation of this agreement or Management's rules and regulations may be deemed by Management to be a breach by Resident. No guest may stay longer than 10 days without permission of Management; otherwise a $10 per day guest charge will be due Management.

(i) Noise: All radios, television sets, phonographs, etc. must be turned down to a level of sound that does not annoy or interfere with neighbors.

(j) Resident shall maintain his own yard and shrubbery and furnish his own garbage can.

(k) Resident's Guide: Management reserves the right at any time and from time-to-time to prescribe such additional rules and make such changes to the rules and regulations set forth and referred to above, as Management shall, in its judgment, determine to be necessary from the safety, care, and cleanliness of the premises, for the preservation of good order or for the comfort or benefit of Residents generally.

ENTIRE AGREEMENT:

25. This agreement and any attached addendum constitute the entire agreement between the parties and no oral statements shall be binding. It is the intention of the parties herein that if any part of this rental agreement is invalid, for any reason, such invalidity shall not void the remainder of the rental agreement.

IN WITNESS WHEREOF, the parties hereto have caused these presents to be signed in person the day and year first above written.

_____   _____

_____   _____
MANAGEMENT   RESIDENT(S)

NUMBER OF RESIDENTS IN THIS PREMISE IS _____

Roommate Shared Rental Agreement

This roommate agreement is intended to protect roommates regarding financial obligations with respect to the rental agreement for property located at

This agreement is secondary to the lease or rental agreement. All roommates are responsible for their own actions with respect to

- Property Care

- General Housekeeping

- Behavioral Standards

- Financial Responsibilities and Obligations

The standards will be what is fair and reasonably set forth by the landlord's expectations and the other roommates.

Any damages to the property are to be taken care of by the party who caused the damage. It is the responsibility of that person to obtain estimates for repair work and make all arrangement to have the repairs made to the expectation of the landlord, including paying for such repairs.

Behavioral misconduct is a terminating offense. If behavior is unacceptable to the other roommates or puts all parties at jeopardy of being asked to vacate the premise by the landlord, the offending roommate can be asked to leave by the other roommates.

All financial obligations are to be split between the following parties as defined:

Date:

Sample Roommate Shared Expense Agreement

Expense Category	Total Amount	Roommate #1	Roommate #2
Rent	$650	$325	$325
Deposit	$650	$325	$325
Electric	Varies	50%	50%
Gas	Varies	50%	50%
Water	N/A	N/A	N/A
Trash	N/A	N/A	N/A
Cable/Internet	$100	$50	$50
Telephone	$50	$25	$25

Roommates Guarantors' Agreement

The Roommate Agreement financial obligation and responsibilities is backed by a guarantee to protect all parties in this agreement. If a roommate does not pay his/her obligation, the guarantor accepts financial responsibility for that roommate

- Rent & services are due and payable on the_____day of the month.

- If monies due are not paid on the date due, the guarantor has five days to respond with monies due.

Roommate Name: ――――――――――――――――――――

Guarantor Name: ――――――――――――――――――――

Street Address: ――――――――――――――――――――

City, State, Zip Code: ――――――――――――――――――――

Phone Number: ――――――――――――――――――――

Roommate Name: ――――――――――――――――――――

Guarantor Name: ――――――――――――――――――――

Street Address: ――――――――――――――――――――

City, State, Zip Code: ――――――――――――――――――――

Phone Number: ――――――――――――――――――――

Roommate Name: ――――――――――――――――――――

Guarantor Name: ――――――――――――――――――――

Street Address: ――――――――――――――――――――

City, State, Zip Code: ――――――――――――――――――――

Phone Number: ――――――――――――――――――――

Sample Shared Utilities/Services Agreement

Rental/Lease Agreement Deposits

A	Cleaning Deposit	$
B	Last Month's Rent	$
C	Electric and Gas Utility Deposit	$
D	Telephone Service Deposit	$
E	Water and Garbage Pick up Deposit	$
	Total Deposit Due	$

Monthly Operating Account

A	Monthly Rent	$
B	Monthly Electric and Gas Bill	$
C	Monthly Telephone Bill	$
D	Monthly Water and Garbage Bill	$
E	Monthly Groceries Bill	$
	Total Monthly Operating Expenses	$

Monthly operating expenses divided by the number of roommates equals each roommate's financial expense obligation

Chapter Four Summary

1. Getting your own place....Where should you start?

- Do you want to live alone and can you afford it

- Do you prefer to share housing with a roommate

2. Types of Housing

- Studio Apartment

- Apartment , Condominium, Duplex or House

- Condominium

- Duplex

- House

- Dorm

3. The Biggest Consideration - Location, Location, Location

- Next to school, work, conveniences

- Neighborhood amenities

4. What's the best type of agreement for you?

- Lease agreement

- Month to Month rental agreement

5. The Application Process

- The rental application

- The walk through and move in inspection

- Shared Rental Agreement

- Roommates / Guarantors

- Financial Agreement

6. Setting Up Utility Services

- Phone

- Gas

- Electric

- Water

- Trash

- Cable

- Internet

- Landscaping if required

Chapter Four Quiz

1. What are your options in terms of living arrangement when moving out for the first time?

2. List four types of living quarters available

3. What should you take into considerations when arranging a shared rental agreement?

4. List two things you should do when completing a rental application?

5. List two types of agreements used when sharing housing with roommates and describe the importance of using such contracts.

6. What two things should you have when setting yourself up in your own place?

7. List three forms that can be used when sharing housing with roommates.

CHAPTER FIVE
BUDGET

Keeping Yourself Out Of Financial Trouble

How To Set Up Your Own Budget

The Credit Rewards Of A Budget

Don't Forget To Pay Yourself

Having Money For The Unexpected

More Money Less Stress

Developing a Budget

A budget is defined as an estimate, often itemized, of expected income and expenses for a given period in the future. In simple words, a budget is a plan of operation utilizing an allotment of funds for a particular purpose.

We can not overemphasize the importance of putting a budget into place and utilizing it. Without a budget, you have no plan of how you intend to manage your income or expenses. Without a plan, you will live with constant impulse and rationalization. It typically does not come to your attention that you need a budget until you are in financial trouble. You realize that you don't have enough money to cover your basic expenses. You may try to understand why you don't have enough money to pay those regular bills. After all, you make enough money, right? Well, without a budget you simply don't know where you are spending your money. That spells trouble.

Estimating your Income

The first step when putting together a budget is to figure out what your income is. For some, this can be fairly simple. If you're paid a salary for the work you do, the amount you receive each pay period will be a constant figure. If you are paid hourly, it may be a bit more difficult to calculate your estimated income. You will have to do a conservative job of estimating the income based to the best of your knowledge on the hours you will be working in any given period. Remember to be conservative when estimating your income rather than liberal. It is better to end up with more income than you planned for, than to end up with less. For those of you who are on some kind of commission only pay structure, it may be even more difficult to know what your projected income will be for a given period of time. For most people, budgeting monthly makes the most sense since most bills are due on a monthly basis and one month is a manageable period of time.

Estimating your Expenses

Next, you will need to know what your expenses will be for the same period of time as you estimated your income. Create a master list of all creditors complete with their name, mailing address, and a telephone number with contact name. There will be some constant expenses paid every month. For example, your housing cost. Then there will be those expenses that vary slightly, such as your electric or gas bill. You may be able to know approximately what the expense will be, but not exactly until the actual invoice comes. In a case such as this, you will want to estimate the figure high. You might want to take the highest historical invoice and use it every month when you budget your income against your expenses. You may be able to go back and do some historical evaluation of the expense based on some variable, such as the month of the year.

Payment Due Dates

Once you have all your estimated costs listed, you will want to put a due date next to each. This would be the latest date that the payment is expected to be received by the creditor and still be considered on time. When you are calculating your budget, plan to pay your bills in advance of the due date. By getting into this habit, not only will you build a good credit rating by making sure that your payments are all made on time, but you are eliminating a lot of stress by not waiting until the last minute. If you wait until the last minute to pay a bill, you risk spending the money on something else. You might jeopardize your utility service, for example. If you don't make the payment on time, the creditor has the right to shut off your service or close your account. If you don't pay your rent, the landlord has the right to evict you, which could leave you homeless. It's simply self-discipline. Do yourself a favor, make this a habit. It will pay for itself many times over during your lifetime.

Including a Percentage for Savings

When calculating your monthly expenses, you will also want to include a portion to be set aside for your savings. As a general rule, financial consultants recommend that you save 5% to 10% of your gross income. It is best to take this amount right off the top before you start spending the income. If you don't do the savings part first, you probably never will. In order to be prepared for some unexpected event, to get ahead, and to plan for your future or retirement, you should be saving a portion of your income every month. You may choose to invest that savings at some point. As for now, just putting it into a savings account can be the first step.

More Income and Less Expense

The number one objective in creating your budget is to earn more than you spend. It is really just that simple. If you earn $2,000.00, you will put $200.00 into savings and have $1,800.00 remaining to pay all your expenses. You simply cannot spend more than the $1,800.00. You should always leave a margin, not spend every last penny of your income. You never know what might come up in the way of expenses. You may have some kind of emergency and need a little extra cash immediately. It is best to have a buffer between your earnings and your expenses. We will spend more time going over this when we get into the section about credit.

Setting up a Tracking System

It will be easier to keep track of your budget if you have some type of a tracking sheet which lists your income and your expenses. There are lots of different ways to set this up. Please refer to the examples at the end of this section.

For those of you who have a personal computer, there are many different software programs available to help you manage your personal finances. These programs do everything from allowing you to record your check register to putting together a debt consolidation plan to maximize every dollar you spend. With a little practice, you can have complete control over your personal finances.

In Conclusion

As we stated earlier in this section, having a budget in place and using it is essential to your financial independence. There are many success stories and many stories of financial disaster. The best thing you could do is establish early on a strong sense of self discipline with regards to managing your hard earned money. That is not to say that you cannot use some of the money you earn for your own personal enjoyment and for recreation and hobbies. Remember, life is a balance. You can balance work with pleasure. It is healthy to have a well rounded life with satisfying work and pleasurable pastimes. Just remember, it is very easy to get into financial trouble if you don't watch yourself every step of the way and discipline yourself when you need to. If you follow this type of a plan, you will have extra money to invest for your future dreams without feeling deprived along the way.

Sample Cash Flow Worksheet

Creditor	Due Date	Payment Amount	Paid Date/ Check No.	Income/ Balance
			January 1, Year	$1,000
Landlord	Month/Day/Year	$400	Date/Check No.	$600
ABC Credit Card	Month/Day/Year	$100	Date/Check No.	$500
Car Payment	Month/Day/Year	$100	Date/Check No	$400
Car Insurance	Month/Day/Year	$100	Date/Check No.	$300
Savings (10%)	Month/Day/Year	$100	Date/Check No.	$200
Food	Month/Day/Year	$100	Date/Check No.	$100
Gasoline	Month/Day/Year	$100	Date/Check No.	$0
			January 15, Year	$1,000

Chapter Five Summary

1. You can stay out of financial trouble by

   • Structuring a budget

   • Understanding and knowing your cash flow

2. Set up your own budget by

   • Estimating your income

   • Estimating your expenses

3. The benefits and rewards of a budget are

   • The ability to stay ahead of your payments

   • It develops self-discipline and self control

4. Pay yourself first before spending by

   • Saving 5%-10% of your income

   • Planning for your future and retirement

5. Have money for the unexpected

   • Unexpected medical expenses

   • Unexpected auto repairs & maintenance

   • Have money set aside in case you should become unemployed

6. You can have more money and less stress by

   • Having money for the unexpected

   • Not having to live from payday to payday

Chapter Five Quiz

1. What is the first tool for staying out of financial trouble? Explain your answer.

2. What two things will you need in order to set up your budget?

3. What are the rewards of having a budget?

4. Who do you pay first, how much, and why?

5. List an example of an unexpected expense.

6. What can your extra money be used for?

CHAPTER SIX
BANKING

Banking Relationships

How To Manage Your Bank Accounts

Keeping Track Of What You Do Daily

Understanding Other Services Of Your Bank

Balancing Bank Statements

Types of Bank Accounts

If you don't already have a relationship with a bank, you will want to establish one by opening some type of an account. It is best to have two accounts, a basic checking account and a savings account. It may be convenient for you to have both accounts in the same banking institution. There are many banks to choose from. You may want to establish an account with a national bank due to the branch locations being all over the country. You may choose to do business with a small locally owned bank for convenience and relationship with their staff. You may wish to find a bank that will offer you a credit card or one that offers investing options. It may be that you want a bank that does commercial loans or home loans for your future plans. Whatever your reasons may be, you will want to establish a relationship with a bank and maintain it for a good length of time. We have discussed in previous sections how the length of time will affect your image of stability.

Most financial advisors recommend that you place between 5% and 10% of your gross income into some form of savings. A savings account at your bank is one way to save money for your future. Most savings accounts are set up on some kind of interest bearing basis. Depending on your balance, there may or may not be a monthly service charge assessed by the bank. If you get in the habit of taking 10% of your gross earnings right off the top before you spend any of your income and place it into some form of savings, before long you will have a nice nest egg set aside for emergency, retirement, or some other goal you may have, such as buying a home. There are many ways to save and to invest money for your future. You may want to meet with a financial consultant to review the many options.

Utilizing a checking account to pay your bills is a very good tool to keep track of your expenses and where your money goes. It is also a good way to provide proof of payment in the event there is a dispute. There is typically a monthly service charge assessed by the bank. Generally, you must also pay the cost of the checks themselves. You can order them through your bank or through private companies. Sometimes banks may offer free checking to certain segments of the population, such as senior citizens or students.

When a payment must be made by mail, a checking account is essential. The check written is basically the same as cash. You must have the funds in the account before you write the check. It is essential that you understand how to avoid writing checks against what is referred to as non-sufficient funds. Writing checks against non-sufficient funds is not only embarrassing, but is very costly and can cause the bank to terminate your account. If your check bounces, it means that there were not enough funds in the account to cover the amount of the check. Normally, if this happens, the recipient of the check will charge you a fee for the inconvenience. Their bank will also charge a fee for having to return the check on behalf of their customer. In addition to that fee, your bank will charge you a fee for having written the check against non-sufficient funds in the first place. Depending on the amount the check had originally been issued for, you may far exceed that amount just in fees associated with committing this offense. Just don't do it. It is much easier to manage the account by using simple math.

When you open your checking account, you will deposit an amount which will become your opening balance. Then, as you write checks against that balance, you will record them in your check register. This will include the check number, the date the check is written, who the check is written to, and the amount of the check. You will then deduct the amount of the check from the balance and record the new balance. On the actual check, you will record the date you are writing the check, the recipient of the check, the amount the check is issued for (written in numerical form), and then that same amount spelled out in words for clarification. You will sign your name as it appears at the bank. Of utmost importance is the section in the lower left corner of the check. This is commonly a line with the word FOR. In this place, you will want to record what this check is being issued for. If there is an account number, you might list it here and make some short notation about what the payment is for. An example might be, "rent due 1/1/00" along with the street address of the property.

When depositing money into the checking account, you will use a deposit slip. On this slip, you record the date of the deposit, the amount of cash you are depositing, any checks which are being deposited along with their amounts, and the total amount being deposited into the account. You should always get a receipt when making a deposit into your account. Always record the deposit amount in your check register and add it to the balance. Please note, when depositing money into your checking account, if you wish to take any cash back from that deposit, there is an area where you indicate that amount, deducting it from the total amount being deposited and you are required to sign the deposit slip for the cash back.

Bank Fees

When managing a checking account, don't forget to include any bank fees assessed to your account. Often, these fees are deducted on a specific date each month. Also, if you order checks through your bank and those checks are not included in the monthly service fee or designated as free, you will need to deduct the charge for the checks in your register. Your bank should be able to tell you the exact cost for a box of checks at the time you order them.

Automatic Teller Machines (ATMs)

Many banks offer their customers Automatic Teller Machine Cards to be used with their accounts. These cards are commonly referred to as ATM cards and can be a very convenient tool for getting cash from your account when your bank isn't open for normal business hours. They can often be used as debit cards at many shops. This can be a great way to get around without carrying cash with you. There are a couple of things you must do when using an ATM card. Always record the amount of cash you are withdrawing from the ATM machine along with any fee being charged for use of that ATM machine in your check register. When using the card as a debit card in some retail facility, you will also need to record the amount of the purchase in the check register. If you fail to do this, you will not be able to balance your statement at the end of the month.

Balancing the Bank Statement

Each month, the bank will send you a statement of your account activity. The statement has a regular cut off date each month. The statement will have a beginning balance shown. This amount should be the same as the ending balance reflected on the previous month's statement. The statement will reflect the total amount deposited into the account during the statement period. It will also reflect the total amount of checks which have been written and have cleared the bank during the statement period. A total of ATM withdrawals will also be listed as will any bank fees such as your monthly service fee. There will be a section where all checks which have cleared your account during the statement period are itemized. This section will show the check number, the date it cleared your bank, and the amount of the check. Sometimes not all checks written will be reflected on the statement. This simply means that they have not cleared the bank prior to the statement cut off date. This does not mean that you should not consider them when balancing your statement.

The first step in balancing your statement is to go through and mark the checks which have cleared your account from your check register. Then you need to calculate which ones have not reflected on the statement. The basic process is to take your beginning balance, add to it the total amount deposited, and subtract the total amount of the checks which have cleared along with the ATM withdrawals and any bank fees. The figure you come up with should match what the bank statement shows as an ending balance. Don't forget to calculate any outstanding checks you have. This will give you your true and actual balance.

Sample Check Registry

Number	Date	Transaction Description	Payment Debit	Code	Fee	Deposit Credit	Balance
Deposit	1/1/10					$1,000.00	
							$1,000.00
101	1/5/10	Electric Company	$85.85				
							$914.15
102	1/5/10	Telephone Company	$125.15				
							$789.00
103	1/5/10	Grocery Store	$50.00				
							$739.00
104	1/12/10	ABC Credit Card	$151.00				
							$588.00
ATM	1/12/10	Cash Withdrawal	$40.00				
							$548.00
105	1/12/10	Auto Insurance	$148.00				
							$400.00
106	1/12/10	Grocery Store	$50.00				
							$350.00
107	1/12/10	Gas Credit Card	$100.00				
							$250.00
108	1/14/10	Cash With-drawal	$100.00				
							$150.00
Deposit	1/15/10					$1,000	
							$1,150.00
109	1/16/10	Grocery Store	$50.00				
							$1,100.00
110	1/20/10	Rent	$500.00				
							$600.00

André J. Olivan Sr.

111	1/25/10	Cable Company	$50.00				
							$550.00
112	1/25/10	Grocery Store	$50.00				
							$500.00
113	1/25/10	Car Payment	$150.00				
							$350.00
Transfer	1/25/10	To Savings Account	$200.00				
							$150.00

Chapter Six Summary

1. Banking Relationships

   - Are critical to your credit future

   - Affect your image of stability

   - Open future opportunities

2. Managing you bank account includes

   - Have a standard savings account in conjunction with your checking account

   - Have the ability to transfer funds in the event of an emergency

   - Manage long-term savings for retirement

3. Banking Transactions help keep track by

   - Managing your daily expenses with your checking account

   - Managing your budget with your checking account

4. Understanding the other services of your bank

   - ATM/Debit Cards

   - Loans

   - Safe Deposit Boxes

   - Different types of financial institutions includes, local, regional, statewide, national and international

5. Balancing statements - easier than you think

- Easier when monitored on a monthly basis

- Keeping receipts of all transactions (Checking, savings, ATM, debit cards)

- Bank charges and outstanding checks

Chapter Six Quiz

1. How does your banking relationship affect you? Explain your answer.

2. What type(s) of bank account(s) should you have and why?

3. List two advantages of the checking account register.

4. List three services most banks offer.

5. How often should you balance your checking account and why?

CHAPTER SEVEN
ESTABLISHING CREDIT

Credit, How It Affects You

Types Of Credit

How Credit Is Determined

Costly Mistakes Of Mismanaging Your Credit

Assets Versus Liabilities

Bankruptcy

Establishing Your Credit

Webster's Dictionary defines credit as permission for a customer to have goods or services that will be paid for at a later date. It also defines credit as, the reputation of a person or firm for paying bills or other financial obligations when due.

We discussed paying bills on time in the section about Budgeting. This is a critical point for discussion. In our society, credit is essential to getting around. Credit can be a wonderful financial tool. It can also lead to financial ruin, depending on how you manage it.

Types of Credit

Credit comes in different forms. Let's take a look at some of the different forms of credit available:

- Secured Credit – a loan taken out against the value of something, for example an automobile. The automobile is the collateral pledged for payment on the loan. If payments are not made, the lender can repossess the automobile. A home loan would be considered a secured debt. There is a specified loan period with monthly payments. There can be a penalty for paying the loan off early. Most often, the interest rate applied to a secured loan will be lower than that for an unsecured loan.

- Unsecured Credit – No collateral specifically pledged in exchange for payment of the loan. Your integrity and credit rating are important in getting an unsecured loan. A personal loan from your bank would be an example of an unsecured note. If you pledge something at the time you take out the loan, (for example, your savings account) then the loan is no longer considered an unsecured debt. There is a specified loan period as on a secured loan with a monthly payment due. Again, there can be a pre-payment penalty assigned for paying the loan in full prior to the end of the loan period.

- Revolving Credit – Unsecured loan amount with a credit ceiling based on income and credit payment history. Revolving credit commonly has a high interest percentage assigned to the balance. The monthly payment amount will vary depending on the balance due. Credit cards are an example of revolving credit. There is no specific term to this type of a loan; it continues indefinitely. You can pay the balance in full or make the minimum payment due or any amount in between the minimum and the balance due. Credit card companies can charge interest on top of previous interest and for this reason; it is not wise to pay only the minimum amount due each month for revolving credit. In fact, it is best to pay credit card balances in full each month to avoid getting into a negative amortizations, meaning you are paying less than the interest being applied to the balance and your debt is increasing rather than decreasing with each payment made.

As we have mentioned, credit is granted upon proving that one is not only credible, but also that one acts with integrity and has commitment. You may wonder how a bank or credit company determines those traits when granting or denying credit. After all, most of the time, they don't even know you. Well, there are ways to prove your credibility and integrity as well as your level of commitment in the eyes of a creditor or prospective creditor. You must remember that a creditor is taking a risk, gambling if you will, that the money they put up front on your behalf will be returned. Since this is business, not personal, the creditor has something to gain. Namely, the creditor stands to make a profit on the money they lend you through the interest charged for the period of time that you are using their money. Let's talk a little about the traits that a creditor is looking for.

- Credibility – defined as resulting from a good reputation

- Integrity – defined as uncompromising adherence to moral and ethical principles; soundness of moral character; honesty.

- Commitment – defined as the act of committing, pledging, or engaging oneself. To pledge or make a commitment to pay bills on time.

So how do we prove to a prospective creditor that we possess all of these desirable traits? Well, we show them through prompt and responsible payment history. We show them through both personal and business references. We show them through stability that is proven by a track record of residency, length of time at a job, the manner in which we care for the things that belong to us, and the manner in which we dress or present ourselves to others. We show them by a proven record of proper personal management that we have commitment, creditability, and integrity.

You may be wondering how to start to establish credit and build a reputation of credibility. It really isn't very difficult to do. You need to understand that our economy is driven by credit. There is a lot of money to be made off of the credit granted to the general population. There are many hidden fees, and unfortunately, most people really don't understand when it might be appropriate to use credit.

If you are young and have never had a loan or credit card, the easiest way to begin to establish credit is through a credit card company. Many credit card companies will issue first time users a secured card which simply means that they will collect a security deposit from you and grant a very low credit limit to start out with. An example might be for a $99.00 security deposit, the credit card company will issue a credit card with a $300 maximum credit limit. As you will see, they are risking $201 if you run the card up to the maximum limit and never make a payment. No prudent person would choose to do such a thing. It spells financial disaster.

Credit Reporting

Creditors report payment information to the three major credit reporting agencies. This information will go on your record for seven years. Bankruptcy is a ten year black mark on your credit. Any time you are applying for any type of credit, even if you are applying to rent an apartment, a credit check is most often run and reviewed as part of the consideration about whether to rent to you or to issue you some type of credit. You will want to look very responsible on these credit reports. So, each time you make your monthly payment on that small credit card, they are reporting you as making a timely payment to the credit reporting agencies. As time goes along and you continue to make your payments timely, the credit card company will probably review your account for a credit line increase. In other words, they will reward you with an increase in the limit you are able to charge on that particular credit card. They might increase it from $300 to say $500. After a while, you may find that you have quite a lot of available credit to use if you should decide to. Other credit card companies will review your type of account and more than likely, they will send you offers in the mail for other credit cards. Some of these may be like your first one. It may require some kind of a security deposit, and others may not require the deposit. When you are reviewing these offers, beware of any hidden charges, such as annual fees. Some companies charge large sums of money each year just to have the charging privilege. Remember something, these companies make a lot of money from their cardholders in interest assessed to their balances. Most credit cards have Annual Percentage Rate of 18.99% or more. Some may offer an introductory rate lower than this, but again, you will want to read the fine print so that you are fully informed about the terms and conditions.

Penalties

Many times, if you pay your monthly statement after the required due date, the company will charge a fee. It can be $25, for example, even if the payment is received only one day after the due date listed on the invoice. This is why it is so very important to pay your bills well in advance of their due date. These companies are not forgiving of the US Postal Service losing a piece of mail or having delays for any reason. It is your responsibility to make sure the payment gets to the company on time and anything less than that you will be penalized for. Setting up your payments in advance to be paid electronically helps prevent your payments from being late.

Should you charge over the limit set by the credit card company, two things can result. It may be that, when you are attempting to make a purchase, your credit card will be declined when the merchant runs it through for authorization. This is a standard procedure by all merchants. In today's world of electronic machines, an authorization code can be transmitted directly from your credit card company to the merchant ensuring that they get their payment against your credit card at the time of purchase. If you are going over the limit set forth on your card, the company may not authorize the purchase. This can be a source of embarrassment as you stand in line with the merchant and are told that your credit card won't go through. On the other hand, sometimes, the company will allow it to go through bumping you up over your charging limit. There is a penalty assessed for this action as well. It, too, can be $25 each time you go above the limit granted by the credit card company. Now you can see how quickly the cost of paying with credit cards goes up.

Costly Mistakes

Now, let's say you have that initial credit limit of $300. It's pretty easy to spend $300 today. Say you make a couple of small purchases and maybe use the card to pay for your gasoline a couple of times. You think you're pretty close to the limit, but decide to use the card to pay for that unexpected meal out. To your surprise, the merchant at the restaurant comes back with your credit card slip simply requiring your signature. The Credit Card Company authorized your purchase. Now let's say that final purchase put your balance due at $302. This is only $2 over the $300 limit. Well, depending on the terms of the credit card (the fine print that is sent out with that cute little plastic card – you know, the stuff no one ever reads), you may have just been hit with a $25 over the limit fee. Now let's say your get paid on the 15th of the month and your credit card statement is due on the 12th. Being the prudent person that you are, you don't dare write a check against your account before you have the money in it. So you wait to mail the credit card payment until the 15th when you get your check. It takes several days for the payment to be received at the credit card company. You are past due. They just assessed you another $25 for being past due. Now you owe $50 more than your statement reflected. Plus, you are paying interest on that $50. That is 16% of the total amount of credit limit you have.

You can see how you can very easily and very quickly get into trouble using this simple little credit card.

Advantages of Credit

Credit was originally designed for the purchase of high-ticket items such as homes, automobiles, or boats. Other uses for credit involve business. Credit enables a business owner to purchase materials, build their products, and then sell them. They could then pay off their credit loan and enjoy the profits afforded by the sale. Thus, they were able to grow their business. For the creditor, there is a tremendous rate of return on their investment. It can be a tool to strengthen not only our individual financial history, but also to strengthen the economy in general. Remember that credit is a gamble and should be handled carefully, reviewed often, and certainly never abused or carelessly handled because the price can be very high if you do mishandle your credit. We'll get into this later in this section.

We've discussed many of the pitfalls of misusing credit cards. You may be asking yourself, "Why would I want a credit card?" Using a credit card is not all bad. If you are responsible and use the credit card knowing that the balance will be due at a certain time, and then budget the full amount due monthly, you will be well on your way to building good credit. There is even an advantage in doing this, it's called float time. Float time is the period from when you make the purchase to the time when they bill you for it. You can use the money for other purposes as long as you are sure that when the statement comes due, you will be ready to pay it in full. It translates into having the enjoyment or use of the product you are purchasing without having to make the payment right when you buy the product. You have the enjoyment of the product before it must be paid for. It goes back to the definition we used at the beginning of this section, permission for a customer to have goods or services that will be paid for at a later date.

Let's discuss some of the things for which we would need to have a credit card. Let's say you need to rent a car for a day or longer. You must have a credit card in order to rent a car. In today's world of internet shopping, you would need to have a credit card in order to order something over the internet. If you are in business for yourself, you might use a credit card to pay for business related expenses in order to keep track of those expenses. In an emergency, a credit card can be very useful tool when you don't have any cash with you. These are a few examples of why you might want to have a credit card. As we discussed earlier, credit cards are one of the easiest ways to establish credit for the first time. We talked about how proper management of those credit cards can lead to an excellent credit rating. With a stable work history and adequate income level, this can lead to even more credit flexibility.

Credit Worthiness

There are other ways to establish credit worthiness. Banks and their loan officers are excellent credit references. We discussed the need for you to establish a relationship with a bank by opening a checking and savings account. By having these two simple types of accounts and maintaining them for a good period of time and not mishandling them in any way, you are again establishing a credit history. There is another way to build credibility with your bank. We talked about putting 10% of your gross income into savings. At some point, that savings can be invested if you want. A certificate of deposit is similar to a savings account. A savings account is completely liquid, which basically means you can go into the bank at any time and withdraw the entire amount in the account. The certificate of deposit is locked up for a period of time for example six months, one year, or more. In exchange for this time commitment, the bank will pay a higher interest rate on the money than in an ordinary savings account. Now let us say that over a period of time you have saved several thousands of dollars. You could put $1,000 of that savings into a certificate of deposit at your local bank branch. After establishing that account for a period of time, you might want to go into the bank and meet with the loan officer. You would discuss with that person taking out a loan in the amount of $1,000 and using the certificate of deposit as security for that loan. Most banks would quickly approve such a proposal. Not only do they have the loan amount secured with your certificate of deposit, but they will be earning interest on the loan amount you are taking out, (in this example, $1,000). You would ask for a loan period of say six months to one year. Within a couple of weeks, you would receive a coupon book for the payments on your new loan. The best thing you could do would be to put the $1000 aside and use it to make the payments on the loan. It would be most beneficial to make the first couple of payments right away, say one or two weeks apart. This puts you in advance of the payment terms outlined when you took out the loan. You then make timely payments for the remainder of the loan period until the loan is paid in full. You can do this at more than one bank. By paying the loan amount back in a more satisfactory fashion than what is required of you, you are earning instant credit worthiness with the bank officers. These are excellent credit references. Once this type of loan has been paid in full, you might want to approach the loan officer and request an unsecured loan, possibly for a lesser amount than the secured loan attached to the Certificate of Deposit.

More than likely, with your history of re-payment of the first loan, the loan officer will more than likely approve such a loan request. As time goes along and you repay this unsecured loan with the bank, you are again gaining more and more credibility. This is another way in which you can build a credit history. Like opening a credit card account, you will need to exercise self discipline in order to not spend the money you have borrowed, but rather to place it in an interest earning account and make timely payments on the loan amount. The little amount of interest that you end up paying, will, in the long run, pay for itself many times over in your ability to obtain credit easily. Remember, as long as you're properly managing credit, it can be a wonderful tool for maneuvering in our society. If you don't use self-discipline and are sloppy about making sure your payments are paid on time, it can financially ruin you.

So, as you can see, credit can be a double-edged sword. Just as easily as you can make it work to your benefit, you can also become a slave to credit and ultimately be financially ruined from it. Don't become a victim of the credit world. Stay in control of your finances.

Debt Ratios

Let's talk a little about debt ratio. Debt ratio is simply the total amount owed in credit against your gross income or earnings. Debt ratio becomes very important when you want to take out a large loan, say, for example, to purchase a home. If you make substantial income and have established credit, but you owe too much in that established credit, a large loan will often be declined. You might wonder why this is so.

Well, when a lender takes a look at you for consideration of a long term, higher loan amount, say for that dream house you have wanted, they look at many factors including your income, your pay history, credit rating, and also debt ratio. If you owe too much money to other creditors, the lender may turn you down. As a rule of thumb, your debt ratio or debt to income ratio should not exceed 30%. This means that all of your combined credit obligations (including the one you may be applying for) should not exceed 30% of your gross income. An example would be if you earn $1000 per month, you would not want more than $300 in total combined credit. When you get into higher percentages, creditors are less likely to approve you. They want to make certain that their money will be repaid without difficulty. Even if what you intend to take the loan out for is going to be secured as collateral against the loan, the lender will still want you to be within a certain percentage of your total income.

Remember, if you have balances which put your debt ratio out of range, even the most excellent credit history won't do you much good. You will need to pay the balances down in order to get your debt ratio back in order. As you can see, there are many areas to managing your credit history. You need to be on your toes in order to make certain you are making this whole credit system work to your advantage.

Using credit all the time puts us in the mindset that we have more money than we really do. Never lose the concept of pulling the cash out of your wallet or purse and paying for some things with the old fashioned green stuff. We need to stay in touch with how much money we are spending. Using credit can have a camouflaging effect.

It is really easy to have no concept of how much money you are spending each month when you whip out the credit cards to pay. You won't actually realize it until you get the monthly statement. This is where a lot of people get into trouble. They didn't realize just how much they had purchased on credit and really didn't budget that amount into their expenses, meaning they are unprepared to pay the balance in full. As we mentioned before, the best way to handle credit is to pay the balance in full each month. You won't pay interest on the amount owed; you are simply getting the float of time on the money you owe, and enjoying the product or service. For those who lose concept of how much they have spent, when that monthly statement comes and they are unprepared to pay the balance in full, they may elect to pay the minimum payment due. This is not a good habit to get in to. By only making minimum payments, you are actually going backward instead of forward in paying debt off. This is not utilizing credit to your best interest.

Assets versus Liabilities

It is far better to have more assets than liabilities. A home is an asset, and is worth something. Property value typically goes up in value as time goes by. There are other assets that actually depreciate in value as time goes along. Automobiles and certain types of equipment are among these types of assets. Over all, you will want to be worth more in assets than you have in liabilities, or debt. There is a saying that more is not always better. If you are considering purchasing something on credit and the value will depreciate, you need to really evaluate your need for that particular purchase. Over time, it will cost you far more to purchase and over time it will be worth less. Ask yourself a few questions before jumping into a credit purchase:

- Do I need this now?

- Can this wait until I can pay for it with cash?

- If I buy this using credit, will I be able to pay it in full in 30 days when my statement comes?

- If I purchase this, will it help me in a positive way?

- Will this purchase help me establish my credit rating or will it jeopardize me by putting my debt ratio out of proportion?

- Do I know what my debt ratio?

- Am I impulsively purchasing?

You may want to go back to the earlier section about making the right decision and put yourself through the exercise of writing out the pros and cons to each of the questions above. If you do decide to purchase on credit, make sure that you are the one benefiting in all areas, not the creditor.

Credit Card Record Keeping

One other important thing about credit cards is to save all your charge receipts throughout the month. Each month when you receive your credit card statement you should match up each receipt with the charges listed on your statement. This is a good habit to get into because merchants, by some means or another, are known to duplicate charges on the statement. If you have a long list of charges it's easy to overlook them. Also, after checking the statement, destroy the receipt copies so no one can find them and steal your credit card number. Stolen numbers can be used for purchases over the internet or phone orders, etc. A good idea is to keep a file of your monthly statements. Merchants will sometimes, by mistake, put a duplicate charge on a statement 3 or 4 months after the original charge was applied to your statement. You can always look back on past statements and find the duplication.

On a final note, when you open up a credit card account, the creditor fully expects you to use it. If the account is left unused for a period of time, the creditor will simply close the account. Make sure you receive a confirming letter from the creditor that the account is officially closed. This is for purposes of keeping your credit report current. On a credit report, it is much more advantageous if you are the one to close accounts rather than the creditor. When creditors close accounts rather than the person holding the account, it implies that there was some type of derogatory activity which resulted in the termination of the account. If the account holder closes an account, they are the ones in control of their credit and it looks better to prospective creditors.

Bankruptcy - Not A Solution

Sweeping reform in bankruptcy laws makes it almost impossible to wash away debt. Historically it was very easy to eliminate debt that was a result of poor judgment and over extension. The older law made it too easy and liberal for people to avoid repaying at least some of their obligations.

The credit card industry, by its mass solicitation for high interest credit cards and other loans, have encouraged irresponsible spending which has landed borrowers in Bankruptcy Court. At one time bankruptcy was a very painful and humiliating experience and people didn't want to do it. Now, persons who are over extended simply wash their debts with no moral conscience. Unfortunately, individuals who have suffered financial emergencies, such as unforeseen medical expenses and unexpected unemployment, have been ignored by the credit industry. Regardless, people seeking bankruptcy protection will have to repay at least a portion of their debts. In recent years, bankruptcy laws have been re-designed to force more debtors out of Chapter 7 in which obligations are essentially erased, and into a Chapter 13 which places debtors on a court-supervised re-payment plan. The new laws puts limits on income and debt ratios that will not allow eligibility for Chapter 7. When accepting these new credit card opportunities, be very careful of the obligations you're accepting. You may not be able to unwind your credit card crisis any longer.

Sample Credit Card Usage Worksheet

Questions to ask Yourself	Yes	No	Reason
Should I charge this?			
Do I need to purchase this right now?			
Do I have the cash to pay for this?			
Can I wait two weeks to purchase this?			
If I charge this, can I pay for it in full within 30 days?			
Will purchasing this benefit me?			
Will charging this help build my credit worthiness?			
What do I already owe in credit card debt?			
What is my current debt to income ratio?			

Chapter Seven Summary

1. Credit is

- Permission for you to have goods or services paid for at a later date

- Your reputation for paying bills and other financial obligations when due

2. The three types of credit are

- Secured credit - collateral pledged for payment of the loan

- Unsecured credit - based on your integrity and credit rating for unsecured loan

- Revolving credit – a limit is set based on your credit history and income

3. Credit is determined by three factors

- Credibility – good reputation

- Integrity – sound moral, character, honesty

- Commitment – committing to pay your bills on time

4. Mismanagement of your credit history can lead to the following consequences

- Credit bureau is notified of delayed payments

- Your credit cards are shut down

- By developing a late payment history, you will destroy your credit privileges

5. Asset versus liability is a measure of your credit health

- Assets are properties owned by you

- Liabilities are the amounts owed by you

6. Bankruptcy - Not an Option

- Marks your credit history for 10 years

- You are no longer allowed to wash away debts (Chapter 7 of Bankruptcy Laws) for mismanaging credit

- Mismanaging credit will require you to pay off your debts through the court system (Chapter 13 of Bankruptcy Laws)

Chapter Seven Quiz

1. Define Credit.

2. List the three types of credit. What are the differences between them?

3. List the three determining factors of credit worthiness.

4. Outline the consequences of not properly managing your credit. Explain your answer.

5. Define Assets.

6. Define Liabilities.

7. Explain what is meant by debt ratio?

8. How does Bankruptcy affect your credit and for how long?

Chapter Eight
Managing Your Medical
Information

Why You Need A Basic Medical Profile

The Difference Between Life And Death

Establish Yourself With A Local Doctor And Pharmacy

Emergency Contacts

Stress - The Silent Killer

Find Your Formula For Managing Stress

Medical Profiles

Everyone should have their basic medical profile outlined somewhere in the event they are injured or become extremely ill. Someone who does not know you may need to step in to administer immediate aid. It could be that you are involved in an auto accident that renders you injured and in need of emergency care. It could be that you fall ill in your home and must be transported to the nearest hospital for emergency surgery. In an event such as this, it would be very beneficial for you to have your medical profile outlined and accessible for the medical professionals who would be administering your emergency care.

In an event such as those noted above, it would be essential that the professionals involved in your care have someone that they could contact to notify of your condition. It would also be essential that they know what medications you currently take, what medical conditions you might have, and what allergies you might have to any medications or other things. It would be helpful and beneficial to have a surgical history as well. Although you might think that this is personal information, it could mean the difference between life and death.

At the end of this section, you will find a sample one page sheet with the basic information which would be helpful in the event of a life threatening emergency. Many calendar or planner books have a page right at the front with emergency information you can complete. This would be helpful only if the persons responding to your emergency had access to your planner.

Another idea would be to complete a form such as the sample facts for life emergency medical information sheet included at the end of this section and place it in an empty plastic pill vial. Label it Emergency Information and put your name on it. You can get a plastic pill vial by going to your local pharmacy and asking for one. Place the vial into your purse, backpack, glove-compartment of your vehicle or in some other easy place. The hope would be that in the event of an emergency, someone would notice the vile and look at it to see if you are taking some type of medication. They would find all the necessary information that a health care professional would find useful in treating you under emergency conditions.

If you have a life threatening condition, such as diabetes or seizure disorder, it would be prudent of you to wear a Medical-Alert bracelet. This is a sure way for the emergency technician to know the most critical information prior to administering any medication or care.

Emergency Contacts

When listing an emergency contact, remember to list someone who can be contacted easily and who can respond to your needs. It might not make sense to list someone who lives across the country from you.

It would be a good idea to list more than one emergency contact. You will want to list their name, address, telephone number, and relation to you. By listing more than one person, in the event the first contact is not accessible, the second or third person might be.

Getting Established with a Health Care Provider

You should also be set up with a regular health care provider. Even if you are extremely healthy, you should have a provider that can be contacted to treat you in the event you become ill. It is much easier to have the registration information and medical history information already on file with the provider. You don't want to complete this information when you don't feel well or when you are in some type of emergency. It would also be a good idea to be registered at your local hospital. If you need to be transferred, especially if you are not conscious, the hospital would be able to pull all the necessary information up and it might assist in the paper process and proper care. Naturally, your health insurance information should always be current.

Pharmacy

Pharmacies are another place where data should be maintained. The pharmacist would have records of any medications you have taken recently and any drug reactions which might be important to know. It is best to use one pharmacy in having any prescription drugs filled for this reason. A pharmacist can be a very knowledgeable resource to you.

Stress

Thus far, we have addressed the issue of handling emergency or unexpected medical issues. Let's not forget about taking care of yourself at all times. Living a balanced life is probably the key to staying healthy. Naturally, you should practice preventative medicine by eating right, getting enough sleep, and exercising to maintain your health. In today's world, you have different types of stress issues that affect your health dramatically. In years gone by, individuals dealt with stress in other ways. Stress can affect your health in a more subtle way and for that reason, it is worth going over the general information.

Physicians have long recognized that people are more susceptible to diseases of all kinds when they are subjected to great stress. Negative events seem to cause enough distress to lower the body's resistance to disease. Even positive events can cause an upset to a person's ability to fend off disease. For example, a new baby in the house can be a very joyful event and at the same time cause the new parents to be so fatigued that they are more susceptible to disease. Scientists have devised a list of life events and rated the relative stressfulness of each. The death of a spouse or parent rates at 100%. Divorce rates at 73%. Going to jail is rated at 63%, whereas being fired from a job rates at 47%, and so on. In today's world, stress may be brought on or worsened by psychological stress. These psychosomatic disorders commonly involve the autonomic nervous system, which controls the body's internal organs. The results can be headache, back and facial pain, asthma, stomach ulcers and high blood pressure.

Although stress can exert some influence on our bodies such as flu symptoms and colds, it can also cause diseases such as tuberculosis, or even cancer. Scientists attribute at least part of this effect to evolutionary history, reasoning that, at one time, people had to live with constant physical threats from wild animals and the elements, as well as from one another. The body developed in a way that it manages these physical stresses. The heart beats faster, blood pressure rises, and other body systems prepare to meet the threat. When a person does something active to cope with a threat, these systems return to normal. Running away or fighting the so-called flight or fight reaction, are both successful ways of coping with many physical threats. Problems arise, however, when the body is prepared, as described, to cope with danger, but can not do so. Being caught in a traffic jam, for example, can cause the body to prepare for a flight or fight response. When no action can be taken, the body's systems remain overly active. Similar repeated experiences of this frustrating nature can lead to conditions such as high blood pressure.

Scientists have been studying a certain type of behavior that is referred to as Type A behavior. This term was originally applied to people who were prone to coronary artery disease. However, the Type A coping style, characterized by competitive, hard-driving intensity, is common in United States society. Mounting evidence indicated that Type A behavior is associated with an increased incidence of several stress-related disorders.

High Blood Pressure, as we mentioned before, is one of the most common disorders that is worsened by stress. It afflicts approximately 20% of the general public. Although high blood pressure has no noticeable symptoms, hypertension can damage the kidneys and can lead to stroke. Other common stress related disorders are gastrointestinal problems, ulcers, and anorexia nervosa. Respiratory disorders can also be affected by stress. Asthma attacks are characterized by wheezing, panting, and a general feeling of suffocation. Emotional stress can aggravate asthma and other conditions such as skin disorders.

Post Traumatic Stress Disorder (PTSD) can be brought on by extremely traumatic events such as accidents, catastrophes, or battles. PTSD may take many months to appear after an initial state of numbness is observed and may involve nervous irritability, difficulty in relating to surroundings, and depression.

Managing Stress

There are as many different methods of dealing with stress as there are people. Find the best way to deal with your own stress and use it. Don't ignore the signs of stress. They could cause serious medical conditions. Your doctor may want you to take some kind of medication. For example, if you are experiencing high blood pressure, it may be recommended that you seek psychological assistance. Exercise is a very useful method of relieving stress, and it releases healing chemicals (Endorphins) in your body to deal with stress. The following are some tips that might help you when stress knocks at your door:

- Keep order in your life.

- Plan ahead.

- Set reasonable goals – both short term and long term.

- Take on your daily activities with the expectation of completing each task.

- Don't overload yourself.

- Tackle each task separately.

- Prioritize by importance.

The reality is that there will always be stressful things to live with on a daily basis. Some people seem to be naturally better at coping with these every day stresses. But that is not an excuse for those that have a little more difficulty coping with stress. Learning to manage the many situations in your life with ease will pay off in better health and better quality of life. Learn to cope early on.

Sample Emergency Medical Information Sheet

Name:	
Address:	
Phone:	
Date of Birth	
Height/Weight:	
Doctor Name and Phone:	
Hospital:	
Insurance Company:	
ID Number:	
Emergency Contact Information:	
Alternate Emergency Contact Information:	
Allergies:	
Major Medical Condition(s):	
Blood Type:	
Date of Last Tetanus Shot:	
Advanced Directive Information:	
Religious Preference:	

Chapter Eight Summary

1. You need a basic medical profile

- In the event of an emergency and you need care

- Doctors need to know unusual medical conditions

- Doctors need to know allergies of any medications, or any other allergic reactions (bee sting, snake bite, etc.)

2. By having facts for life medical information, you are providing your doctor with

- Medical history

- Family history

- Allergies to medications

3. Establishing a local medical provider and pharmacy

- A local provider may send for your previous medical history for an updated file

- With current medical information at hand it will prevent you from having a medical mishap during an emergency

4. Have emergency contact information available

- List family or friends

- List your medical provider numbers

5. Physicians recognize that stress can cause disease and other illness such as

- High blood pressure

- Internal organ disorders

- Heart problems

- Cancers

- Tuberculosis

6. Stress Management is the best formula

- Keep order in your life

- Don't overload yourself

- Prioritize by importance

- Exercise (most useful method) releases endorphins in your body

Chapter Eight Quiz

1. List two reasons for having a basic medical profile.

2. By having a basic medical profile, what three things are you providing emergency personnel?

3. List three types of contacts you should include in your emergency contact list.

4. List five causes of stress.

5. What is the most useful stress management technique?

CHAPTER NINE
DUTIES TO SOCIETY

Citizens Of The United States Have Two Duties

Voting Is A Privilege

Jury Duty Is An Honor

The Price We Have Paid

Our Freedom Depends On Us

The Privilege of Voting

Suffrage is defined as, the right to vote, esp. in a political election. As citizens of the United States of America, we have the right to cast our vote in elections. Our voice is counted along with the other members of the voting population. We vote our public officials into office. We vote to adopt or reject various laws. It is an honor to vote.

Suffrage dates back to ancient times. In the cities and States of Greece, all free men, who were a minority of the population, were expected to take part in the government of their city. In Rome, the common citizens were granted the right to elect tribunes to intercede for them when they felt that they had been unjustly treated by the government.

It wasn't until the 17th and 18th centuries that the idea of the people under a government having a voice in selecting their leaders gained substantial support. Philosophers of the Enlightenment argued that self-government was a natural right of every person and that governments derive their just powers from the consent of the governed.

This idea influenced the modern view of suffrage, but not to the point of completely eliminating the view that suffrage is a political privilege that is granted by law and is subject to qualifications. The trend of modern governments has been to liberalize the qualifications for suffrage, but many still apply some restrictions besides the obvious standards of citizenship and minimum age. The age restrictions range between eighteen and twenty-one years. In a few countries women still do not have the right to vote. Literacy is often a qualification and in many countries persons convicted of serious crimes are deprived of their voting rights.

The United States Constitution originally specified that each state would determine the qualifications for its voters, however, amendments to the Constitution have prohibited any state from denying suffrage to any citizen by virtue of race or sex or to require the payment of a poll tax as a condition for voting in a national election. Prior to the 1970's, the age limit for voting in the majority of states was twenty-one, although Georgia, Kentucky, Alaska, and Hawaii had lower age limits. The United States Supreme Court in 1970 ruled that eighteen-year-olds had the right to vote in federal elections. The 26th Amendment to the Constitution was ratified in 1971 affording suffrage to eighteen-year-olds in all elections. The right to vote if convicted of a felony varies by State.

Some states required voters to pass literacy tests. However, in 1964, in some states only half of the population was registered to vote in the national election of that year. This led to the Civil Rights Act of 1965, which barred literacy tests and other devices to determine qualifications in states where less than half of the population was registered to vote. In 1970, amendments to the Civil Rights Act banned state literacy tests and also required that ballots be printed in languages other than English in areas where a substantial minority of the local population is literate in another language.

Duty to your Country

The United States is one of the few countries in the world where the citizens are allowed to elect their leaders to represent their viewpoints. It is your duty, as a citizen of the United States of America, to vote for the candidate of your choice. Many wars have been fought and men have died so that you can vote and have freedom of choice. It is your duty to your country to be informed about the issues and to cast your vote on election-day. Your vote counts. Consider the Presidential election of the year 2000, Bush vs. Gore, where only 357 votes decided the President of the United States.

Jury Duty

When you register to vote, you automatically are placed in a pool of citizens whose names can be drawn for jury duty. A Jury is a body of people who are chosen to decide the truth of factual evidence in an action or legal proceeding and, on instruction of the court, to apply the law to the facts. Such a body is called a petit jury or trial jury. An individual can not be convicted of a crime unless a jury of their peers has tried them. Traditionally, a trial jury consists of twelve people, often with one or two alternates.

The exact origin of the jury system is not known. Various writers have attributed it to different European people who at an early period developed methods of trial not unlike the early jury trials in England. It seems probable that the jury in England was derived by sworn inquest. Twelve knights were chosen to serve as recognizers. Their duty was to inquire into various matters of interest to the new rulers of England that might be the subject of public inquiry. These matters of interest would have included the taxation of a subject.

Selection of the Jury

In the United States, the selection of a jury commences when a large group of citizens is called to appear for jury duty at each term of court. These individuals are selected according to statutory and constitutional provisions. Each state has its own qualifications for those who may serve on a jury. In general, all jurors must be United States citizens, local residents, of majority age, of approved integrity, and of reasonable intelligence. The group of jurors called at any one time is known as a panel. Both the state and the federal courts have independent lists of jurors that are made up under the direction of officials known as commissioners of jurors. Jurors are paid, as provided by statute, for the time spent serving on jury duty. It isn't very much money.

At the trial, the selection of the jury is made subject to the direction of the presiding judge. The names of the prospective jurors are drawn by lot by the clerk of the court. Both the defense and the prosecution may examine the jurors to ascertain whether circumstances exist that might improperly influence a juror's decisions, such as a bias or self-interest. The parties to the action or their attorneys may then exercise their right to eliminate undesirable members from the jury by means of challenge.

After a satisfactory jury has been drawn, the jury is sworn in and the trial begins. In general, during the trial, all questions of law are determined by the court and questions of fact are determined by the jury. The weight and credibility of the evidence admitted are determined by the jury.

After all the evidence has been presented, the two counsels first for the defendant and then for the plaintiff or prosecution sum up. This means they each address the jury, reviewing the evidence in the case and commenting on it in a manner favorable to that counsel's side of the case. The judge then makes a charge to the jury. The charge is a statement of the rules of law applicable to the evidence in that particular case. It is given in order to aid the jury in rendering a correct verdict. The jury then retires from the courtroom to begin deliberations. These deliberations continue until an agreement as to the verdict is reached or until the presiding judge deems that the jury can not reach an agreement. When this happens, it is referred to as a hung jury. In the event of a hung jury, a new trial may be called. All members of a jury must agree on a verdict, which in a civil trial may be for the plaintiff or for the defendant and in a criminal trial guilty or not guilty. In some states, the verdict in a civil trial need not be unanimous. In a civil trial, the jury is then empowered to set the amount of the damages. The verdict of a jury is decisive and can not be disturbed unless rendered contrary to law or against the weight of evidence. In a case such as this, the verdict may be set aside, either by the presiding judge or later on appeal.

As you can see, jury duty is serious business. As a citizen of the United States of America, it is your responsibility to vote and to be informed about important issues pertaining to law. It is also your responsibility to serve on a jury should you be summoned and selected to do so and to render a verdict that is true and correct. When you think about it, this is a very small price to pay for the many freedoms we enjoy in our country. When weighed against all the opportunity we have here, this is but a small sacrifice of time.

Chapter Nine Summary

1. Duties to Society

   • Voting

   • Jury Duty

2. Voting goes back to ancient times of free societies

   • Greeks and Romans

3. Voting is a privilege and the United States has paid a high price for it

   • We have fought many wars to keep our constitutional right to vote

   • Hundreds of thousands of your men and women have given their lives to maintain our free society

4. In some States, the right to vote can be revoked if:

   • You are a convicted felon

5. Jury duty is an honor in our free society

   • There is no jury duty in societies with dictatorship or oppression

   • Our country is rich in history of trials by jury

   • Its an honor to be selected as a juror

6. A Jury is a body of persons who are chosen to

   • Review factual evidence in a trial

   • There are 12 persons that make up a jury

   • Render a vote of innocent or guilty by the prosecution or defense

Chapter Nine Quiz

1. Identify two duties to society

2. What two ancient civilizations practiced voting?

3. Give an example of how the right to vote can be revoked.

4. What is a jury?

Chapter Ten
Balancing Responsibilities

Managing Your Financial Obligations

Prioritizing Means Financial Survival

Re-evaluating Your Financial Condition

Financial Emergencies

Mental Peace Of Mind

Avoiding Disaster

Prioritizing

Prioritizing is a very important factor in managing your financial obligations. There are certain survival needs that are essential and must be managed first. Thus, prioritizing becomes an essential part of managing your life.

We discussed budgeting, housing, transportation, and credit in earlier sections. Assuming you have all of these expenses and have figured them all into your budget plan, there is one more consideration. That consideration is the prioritizing of all these important expenses.

Let's take a look at some of the expenses:

- Housing

- Transportation

- Food and Personal Items

- Utilities

- Gasoline

- Telephone

- Insurance Premium

- Credit Obligations

Obviously, you will want to prioritize payment on some of these items before others. Let's look at some of the expenses and imagine the consequences for not paying them. By doing so, you are able to prioritize the payments. As with all things, nothing stays the same forever. For that reason, you should always have a back up plan and be willing to re-evaluate your financial condition in order to update it depending on changing circumstances such as loss of a job or death of a spouse, for instance.

- Housing – Shelter is of utmost importance to our existence. Without it, we are basically homeless. There are too many homeless people in America today. Many of those people would never have imagined that it could have happened to them. Remember, much of the population lives paycheck to paycheck. They have no cushion in the event something interrupts their earnings. Always make sure that you are current or even a little ahead on your housing expense. By doing so, you will have a buffer of time in the event you have to reorganize yourself as a result of loss of your income. If you own your home and you get three months or more behind on your payments, the lender will step in and repossess your home. Not only will this be very damaging to your credit, but could potentially render you homeless. Housing should always be at the top of your list of priorities as far as payments go.

- Transportation – getting where you need to be is quite important especially if that involves getting to your place of employment. If you can't get to work, you more than likely won't get paid either. So, the expense of transportation, whether it be your own automobile, or some rapid transit form of transportation, is vitally important to your survival. You will want to place this expense right up there with housing.

- Food and Personal Items – If you don't nourish your body with good healthy food, you won't be able to function in any form. If you didn't eat at all, you would eventually die. You also need certain personal items to assist with your personal hygiene. These items would also be important items to prioritize in your budgeting and managing of your financial obligations.

- Utilities – Electricity, water, and cable television, are all luxuries that you often take for granted. You might be able to live without electricity for a period of time, but you would certainly die if you had no water. Cable television is a pure luxury item. Certainly, you might not have all the channels you enjoy watching in your spare time, but you could definitely live without it. Some utility payments would rank up there on the list of priority while others would not.

- Gasoline – If you own your automobile and use it to get to and from work, gasoline expense is critical. You can't go too far without it. If you have another means to get around, gasoline expense could be placed as less of a priority, but if you rely on your vehicle to get to and from your place of employment, gasoline will be one of those items to prioritize.

- The Telephone – Certainly, most of you enjoy having a telephone in your home. Is it essential to your survival? Probably not. Telephone expense can get out of control if you're not paying close attention. Long distance charges or cellular telephone bills can eat up your income. This might be an expense you put at the bottom of your list of priorities.

- Insurance Premiums – These are the four basic insurance policies needed.

1. Insuring a home is a requirement of the lender.

2. Insurance on your vehicle is a requirement of the state.

3. Life Insurance is a necessity for your estate.

4. Health Insurance is necessary for your medical needs.

- Credit Obligations – Any unsecured debt obligations if left unpaid will certainly damage your credit. They may not, however, affect your ability to survive. When evaluating the most important things to pay, credit cards might have to stand in line.

Following your budget and prioritizing payment based on your ability to survive will afford you the following:

- Financial Security

- Mental Peace of Mind

- Continuous Credit Building

- Credit Debt in Order of Importance

- Investment for your future

Flexibility

Remember that all things change from time to time. Nothing ever stays the same forever. Don't be fooled into thinking that if you are doing really well today, that it will always be that way. Plan for that rainy day. Always evaluate your current situation and have a plan in place at all times. Be flexible with that plan when it is necessary. There is no guarantee that you will always have your health or that you will always have that good paying job. There are too many sad stories about good people who, due to bad planning or no planning at all, are now members of the homeless community. It doesn't seem to matter what the background has been, life has an interesting way of dishing out unexpected circumstances which challenge your ability to stay on your feet. Learn how not to panic, but to take a proactive position as to your situation, and you will see that the outcome can be very positive.

The Emergency Patch

Remember, sometimes circumstances change and some things might be out of your control If you find yourself in a bind, remember to communicate with your creditors and others in your life. People will have more of a tendency to work with you through a difficult and unexpected situation if you keep the communication channels open. Don't ignore the calls. Face the situation and be proactive. You will work your way through it.

Chapter Ten Summary

1. Prioritizing your financial obligations

   - Prioritizing becomes an essential part of managing your life

   - Prioritizing your finances

2. Prioritizing means Financial Survival

   - Housing

   - Gasoline

   - Transportation

   - Telephone

   - Food

   - Personal Items

   - Insurance Premiums

   - Utilities

3. Re-evaluating your financial condition

   - Survival is based on your priorities

   - Circumstances always change

4. The Emergency Patch

   - When experiencing an emergency, let your creditors know

   - Let them know the severity & circumstances of the emergency

   - Willingness to make partial or interest payments during the emergency keeps your creditors informed.

Chapter Ten Quiz

1. List four typical financial expenses.

2. When re-evaluating your financial condition, what always changes and why?

3. What should you do when you are experiencing a financial emergency?

4. What is the most important part of managing your financial expenses? Why?

CHAPTER ELEVEN
REAL ESTATE - OWNING
YOUR OWN HOME

The Time To Establish Excellent Credit Is Now

From Shelter To A Growing Asset

Internal Revenue Helps To Pay For Your House

Growth From The Depression To The 21st Century

A Springboard For Wealth

Security For You And Your Family

How Credit Impacts your Ability to Buy Real Estate

If there was ever a time to have excellent credit, it would be at the time you decide to purchase a home. Not only is your credit rating essential, but so is your level of income, length of employment, banking relationships, and debt to income ratio. These are all factors in getting a loan for that dream home you are hoping for. Being a property owner opens new credit opportunities to you. Owning property can be one of the best investments you can make. Property typically escalates in value and over a period of time, a profit is normally seen. History shows us that some of the most successful individuals in our country's history have made their fortunes with real estate. Many of them started out with one piece of property and leveraged their way into becoming landlords with multiple dwellings. Don't let the housing crisis of the first decade in the 21st century fool you. Historically, real estate has been one of the best investments and offers one of the best rates of return.

A Little History about Housing

Because basic shelter is essential to everyone, the task of providing adequate housing has long been a concern for not only the individual but also for government. The issue of housing is really inseparable from social, economic and political development.

The United States Census Bureau defines a housing unit as a house, apartment, group of rooms or a single room, occupied or intended for occupancy as separate living quarters. It also has direct access to the unit from the outside or through a common hall and includes a complete kitchen facility. Transient or institutional accommodations and barracks for workers are not counted as housing units.

From the beginning of civilization, attention has been paid to the form, placement, and provision of human habitation. The earliest building codes, specifying structural integrity in housing construction began long ago. City planning activities during the Greek and Roman empires centered almost exclusively on the appropriate placement of urban housing from the perspectives of defense and water supply. These same concerns continued throughout the Middle-Ages. In

13th century Europe, the city became a center of trade, and its walls provided a safe haven from nomadic warriors and looters.

As time went along, the demand for housing increased. For centuries, unplanned additions and subdivision of the existing structures filled the demand. In places where the weather wasn't too harsh, squatting was common, but provided only temporary shelter. Squatting still exists today in the form of homelessness. Vacant land might quickly become a site for makeshift homes set up for the homeless.

By the 19th century, with the Industrial Revolution, people were moving to cities in unprecedented numbers. Workers lived in sheds, railroad yards, and factory cellars, typically without sanitation facilities or water supply.

Demand for Housing

In the post-industrial society of the 20th century, housing in developing nations and poor parts of developed countries continued to be of insufficient quality and did not meet the demand of some parts of the population. Vacant, abandoned central city housing existed alongside structures that were usable but overcrowded and functionally obsolete.

Today, there exists both a demand for housing and a supply of reusable structures that are going unclaimed. This situation is a good example of the complex role housing plays in society. The primary function is to serve the need for shelter and privacy. But now, housing must also offer other advantages such as proximity to the workplace, shopping, businesses, schools, and other homes. It must also offer environment, that is, the quality of the neighborhood, including public safety and aesthetics. It should also offer investment potential.

The physical stock of housing in the United States is one of the nation's principal capital assets. In the United States, about two-thirds of the population lives in single-family dwellings, most of which have been built by small, private housing developers on separate lots. America's housing industry is a largely unorganized group of entrepreneurs who construct housing in their own geographical area. They decide on the type of housing that will be best accepted by the consumers and then proceed to provide this housing through the development process. This is not to say that the independent building industry is completely unregulated. There are various laws, institutions, and public agencies that work to ensure that private-market housing is produced safely by builders and delivered efficiently to consumers.

The quality and the type of housing are controlled by zoning laws. The quality of the housing and the inclusive services to be offered are determined by building or housing codes. Financing needed to construct and purchase housing is available from lending institutions whose activities are governed by law. Consumers are afforded access to this housing through a variety of settlement procedures and fair-housing laws.

Housing has expanded in an outward progression, starting in major cities, and then progressing outward, first following railroad and trolley lines, and then automobile paths such as major roads and interstate highways. Housing in the city was generally either of the single family nature, built primarily as a framed structure on an individual lot, or a multifamily dwelling, built primarily of masonry and having multiple separate units on one single lot of land. Today, there are condominium units, apartment units, duplex and triplex units, single family houses, and huge estates built on large parcels of land. In the last twenty years, modular housing has become increasingly popular because it is inexpensive and easy to construct. Certainly, housing styles vary depending on what part of the country you might be looking at.

Growth of suburban housing in the United States began in the 1920s but was stalled by the Great Depression of the 1930s and certainly by World War II (1939-1945). In the post-war era of the 1950s, a tremendous surge occurred in the suburban housing market. Single family homes on relatively small lots were built in large tract developments. These tracts were built near metropolitan areas and encroached on former farmlands. The growth of housing created significant demands for schools and other public services in these locations. This stimulated the economy in many different ways.

As of 1990, more than 105 million housing units, with a combined market value exceeding $4.1 trillion existed in the United States. Approximately 102 million were year-round housing units. Of these, about 60% were occupied by owners, and 40% by renters. The sixteen Southern states contained more than one third of all housing units. The twelve Midwestern states contained slightly less than one-quarter and the nine Northeastern and thirteen Western states each contained about 20% of the nation's housing. In a robust construction year, a net 1.5 million units might be added to the housing inventory. This was the result of 2.1 million new units added and 600,000 units lost due to natural disaster, highway clearance, or abandonment.

Housing in the United States varies significantly in type, age, value, and quality. Currently, 66% of all U.S. housing consists of single-family homes; another 10% is made up of two-four unit structures; 17% is made up of structures of five units or more; and the remaining 7% of housing consists of mobile homes.

Nearly 22% of the U.S. housing stock was built before 1940; another 57% has been constructed since 1960. In 1990, the median price of a new one-family home was more than $122,900; the average rental was about $489 monthly. More than 72% of the privately owned housing had at least six rooms; rental housing on the average had four rooms. America has become obsessed with super sizing everything. By 2005, the average home was 15% larger in size than the year before.

The federal government was first induced to regulate housing when the nation entered World War I in 1917. This event sparked the expansion of defense plants, thus straining the housing supply for war workers at particular locations. To handle this problem, Congress formed the U.S. Housing Corporation, which remained in existence until the end of the war in 1918. Prior to that there was the establishment of housing codes which regulated the physical conditions and maintenance standards of apartment houses in major cities. Around the turn of the century, a more sophisticated and elaborate code was adopted and more cities joined in to regulate housing. The result is that relative quality of American housing today is exceptionally high. Less than 2% of year-round housing units lack plumbing; only about 3% have more than one person per room (an index of overcrowding); and only about 1% lack exclusive use of kitchen facilities.

The Great Depression

A housing boom occurred in the United States during the 1920s, but activity plummeted during the Great Depression in the 1930s. This prompted dramatic federal housing programs. In 1933, the Homeowners' Loan Corporation was formed to refinance existing home loans. In 1934, the Federal Housing Administration was founded. The FHA, as it is commonly referred to, insured residential loans and thus encouraged lenders to offer long term mortgages, some up to twenty or thirty years at a fixed rate of interest. The FHA housing activity received further support when the Federal National Mortgage Association (FNMA) was created in 1938. The FNMA purchased FHA insured loans, thus establishing an important secondary market and created an avenue for which savings and loans could turn over loans with ease for liquid assets.

Also established in the 1930s was a public housing program, which provided slum clearance and low-cost housing for the poor. These activities were implemented by local housing authorities that received federal financial assistance. This stimulated the housing activity in the late 1930s; however, World War II brought new construction to a halt.

The Post War Era

In the late 1940s and early 1950s, the federal government began adding new programs. In addition to the FHA, FNMA, and the public housing supports, the Veterans Administration began offering guaranteed home loans, obtained by veterans through a program authorized in 1944. This along with the FHA insurance, encouraged development of the postwar suburban land subdivisions which we discussed earlier in this section

The most significant programs, however, of the postwar period were the numerous housing acts providing subsidies for slum demolition, rental housing rehabilitation, and low-income home ownership. The Housing Act of 1949 authorized urban renewal of slum areas. Under this act, local redevelopment authorities purchased and demolished deteriorated properties and then sold the cleared land to private developers for a nominal sum of money. The goal of the Urban Renewal

Program was to replace slum areas with new residential and non-residential units. The program was criticized as a strategy that overemphasized demolition at the expense of viable neighborhoods and to the detriment of poor or minority residents.

By the 1960s, the federal government had changed its housing involvement. The emphasis was shifted from demolition to rehabilitation. In addition, new and expanded housing subsidies were provided for poor and minority households. The Housing Act of 1965 created a program that made subsidies available for low-income and moderately low-income rental units. It also fostered home ownership for the poor. The housing needs of inner city areas were not being met by specially targeted subsidies.

The best-known subsidy plan was the model cities program. The Model Cities Program was authorized in 1966 by the Demonstration Cities Act that focused on upgrading the physical as well as the social aspects of inner city areas. The federal housing efforts were administered by The Department of Housing and Urban Development also referred to as HUD. HUD was created in 1965. In addition to the urban programs, HUD was also in charge of aiding what was referred to as new towns. New towns were self-contained communities which incorporated both residential and non-residential uses.

The 1970s and 1980s

Once again, problems began to emerge in the housing programs in the 1970s. Subsidized rental projects were foreclosed. Single family units, bought by the poor, were abandoned by their owners. Several of the privately developed, publicly assisted new towns experienced near or actual bankruptcy. These conditions caused a moratorium on further subsidies. Assistance began to take the form of block grants. The Community Development Block Grant (CDBG) is a program that was authorized by the Housing Act of 1976, and was a more broad-based housing subsidy. It provided blocks of money for coordinated urban revitalization. The allocation of block grants was a primary redevelopment approach in the 1980s. It has since been significantly reduced.

In the 1980s, the emphasis once again shifted. The emphasis went from rebuilding the direst neighborhoods to improving the so called gray areas that were just beginning to decline. Also during the 1980s, HUD halted construction of new subsidized low-income housing. It seemed that it would be more cost effective to rehabilitate and preserve existing structures than to build new ones. In many cities, private ventures were encouraged to renovate. Unfortunately, none of these actions served to help the poor people and the housing shortage worsened.

The 1990s

In many parts of the United States, the 1990s brought a shortage of affordable housing for the poor and for some low-income and middle-income wage earners. Both rental and owner occupied homes have been affected. Homeless people were living in shelters or on the streets, especially in the cities. At the same time, residential buildings, both private and public, were being abandoned in some crime-ridden neighborhoods. Most inner cities were losing population as the suburban areas continue to be chaotically built. One new trend was the growth of housing being developed to meet the needs of the disabled as well as the elderly. As the majority of the population continues to age, there will be more of a demand for housing that meets the needs of the elderly.

By The Year 2010

By 2010, America had seen yet another real estate crisis. With sub-prime lending rampant and a failing world economy, many over extended Americans found themselves unable to pay their mortgages and bank foreclosure was unprecedented. President Obama introduced a housing loan re-modification program to help families keep their homes

Federal, state, and local governments continue to search for solutions to our housing problems. Proposals include rehabilitating public housing, selling subsidized units to tenants, organizing public-private partnerships, amending zoning restrictions, and issuing housing vouchers. Progress has already been made in the area of factory-built housing, offering the hope that inexpensive homes might be mass produced.

Although each decade seems to bring with it a new approach to solving the never ending dilemma of housing, one thing remains constant; there will always be a need for housing and if you plan for it, you too can share in the American dream.

Chapter Eleven Summary

1. When you decide to purchase your own home, you are going to need the following

- Excellent credit rating

- Continuous income

- Sufficient length of time with employer

- Banking relationship

- Proper debt to income ratio

2. The transition from renting to buying a home creates a growing asset

- When renting, you pay for shelter with no return on monthly rent

- When buying a home, you're paying for shelter, and it increases in value over time

3. Internal Revenue pays for your house

- The interest portion of your house payment is fully tax deductible

- In the beginning of your house purchase, 99% of your payment is interest only

4. Booming growth from the Great Depression to the 21st Century

- The Depression years, 1934, the Federal Housing Administration (FHA) was founded.

- In 1965, the Housing Act was created to make available low income and moderately low income rental units.

- In 1938, the FHA housing activity received further support when the Federal National Mortgage Association (FNMA) was created

- The Department of Housing and Urban Development (HUD) was created in 1965

5. A springboard for wealth

- Federal Housing programs have promoted the development and purchases of homes in the last 50 years

- With tax advantages and the appreciation of your home, you can now build a personal estate

6. Security for You and Your Family

- Having and owning your own home gives you tremendous psychological security

- The equity in your home will allow you to expand and purchase other properties for future investments

Chapter Eleven Quiz

1. When purchasing your own home, identify five things you will need.

2. When buying your own home, what are you paying for?

3. How does the Internal Revenue Service help you pay for your home?

4. What does FHA mean?

5. What does HUD mean?

6. What does FNMA Mean?

7. What does VA mean?

8. When were Federal Housing programs established?

CHAPTER TWELVE
SERVING YOUR COUNTRY

The Privilege Of Living In The United States

The Price This Country Has Paid

History Of The Draft To Voluntary Military

The Honor To Serve Your Country

The Many Benefits Of Serving In Our Military

The Honor of Serving Your Country

We as citizens of the United States are privileged to live in a free country. The opportunities available to each one of us are endless. Many of us take for granted the many freedoms we enjoy as citizens of the United States of America. Many of us do not fully understand the price that our forefathers paid to afford us such luxury and freedom. We must always protect our free world. We must always protect mankind from oppression. For that reason, our government budgets mass amounts of money for the maintenance and development of our armed services.

Prior to 1973, there was some form of conscription for enlistment in our various military branches. Conscription is defined as compulsory enrollment of persons for military or naval service; draft. In 1973, the Secretary of Defense announced that the use of military draft had ended. In 1980, a system of registration was implemented requiring 18-year old men to register only. This was a non-compulsory military registration. In other words, all 18-year old men are registered in the event that a military draft ever becomes necessary, creating a database with eligible men to fill the ranks. The Selective Service System keeps track of the registration date for all 18-year old men, and The Selective Service System has regional offices throughout the nation. The system is headed by a director, appointed by the President with advice from the Senate. The function of the Selective Service System is to be prepared to supply the armed forces with sufficient personnel to ensure the security of the United States. At the present time, enlistment in any branch of the armed services is on an all voluntary basis.

Military service is a fundamental obligation of citizenship dating from early times. In ancient Greek Cities and States, young men were required to serve several years in the citizen militia. In the Roman Republic, compulsory service in the militia was regarded as a privilege. All male citizens between the ages of 17 and 60 served without pay. The older men had restricted duty.

Benefits of Serving Your Country

In addition to the honor of serving your country, a choice to join one of the branches of the armed services also promotes a life habit of discipline. There are certainly numerous areas of training. Other benefits of a military service might include

- lifelong friends

- college education

- career training

- extensive travel opportunity

- health care

- Veterans Administration guaranteed home loans

A visit with your local recruiting officer can open a world of opportunity and possibility for you to advance in an honorable career with the military. You can have excellent job skills and an education after serving your country. There are so many reasons why you should consider joining one of the branches of our armed services.

Chapter Twelve Summary

1. The privileges of living in the United States of America

   - The United States is a Country made up of immigrants from many countries

   - You have the choice to choose a career and build a future for your family, no matter what ethnic group you're from

2. The price this country has paid

   - The United States is the most powerful country in the world today

   - There is no other country that has the freedom that we have in the United States of America

   - Since our independence as a country, thousands of men and women have given their lives so that you can have the freedom that you have today

3. Compulsory military and voluntary military

   - Military service before 1973 was mandatory, and was referred to as The Draft

   - Today, participation is voluntary

   - All 18 year old men are required to register in the event that the military draft becomes necessary

4. It is a privilege and honor to live in this country and it is an honor to serve and preserve our freedom

   - There is a great feeling of honor in serving your country

   - Anyone wearing a uniform of the U.S. military should feel very proud

5. Other benefits to serving in our military include:

- Lifelong friends

- College education

- Career training

- Extensive travel opportunity

- Health care

- VA guaranteed home loans

Chapter Twelve Quiz

1. Name one privilege that comes with living in the United States of America

2. When did Military drafting end and what caused it to end?

3. List six benefits to serving in the military.

Chapter Thirteen
Understanding Taxation

History Of Income Taxation

Your Personal Income Tax Responsibilities

Our Complicated Social Economic System

Social Security Taxes

Understanding The Basic Tax Forms

History of Income Taxation

Income tax is a tax levied by a government on the income of individuals and business firms. Taxes on personal income and business profits are a major revenue sources for most non-communistic industrialized nations. They play a growing role in the tax structures of many developing countries as well. In the United States, personal and corporate income taxes have, in recent years, accounted for more than 60% of the total general tax revenues (not including special purpose levies on wages such as social security).

Because the United States Constitution originally enacted and prohibited the federal government from levying direct taxes, except in proportion to population, a constitutional amendment was required to give full legal sanction to federal use of an income tax. With the ratification in 1913 of the 16th Amendment to the constitution, the United States joined numerous other nations in taxing income.

An individual is required to file an income tax return with the Internal Revenue Service if his or her gross income is greater than the statutory minimum. For federal tax purposes, the term gross income includes wages and other compensation for personal or professional services such as gains from trade, business, dealings in property and securities, and interest and dividends.

An individual tax applies progressive rates, that is, higher percentages for higher incomes, to taxable personal income. A corporate tax, with a less progressive rate structure taps corporate profits. The specific provisions and the impact of both taxes, however, have undergone major changes. The income tax was originally used for taxing the wealthy with very high exemptions. In 1939, it reached only five percent of the population. During World War II, the individual income tax developed into a primary revenue source, drawing from all but the lowest level of income recipients. This resulted from a sharp drop in exemptions combined with rising income levels. Increases in rates further added to the revenue yield. Legislation passed in 1943 allowed for withholding of tax at the source and greatly increased taxpayer compliance. In other words, the employer began withholding the taxes on behalf of the employee. Rapid inflation from the mid-1970s to the early 1980s further broadened the tax base.

Personal income tax returns for the previous calendar year are due on or before April 15. Every corporation subject to taxation, regardless of its income, is required to file a return. During the year, an employer must withhold the taxes due on the wages of employees and pay such taxes to the United States Treasury. Withheld tax is credited against the employee's total liability as computed on the final return. A refund is made to the employee in cases of excess withholdings. A declaration of estimated annual income tax liability must be filed by self employed persons and those that have substantial income not subject to withholding taxes. Estimated taxes are paid to the Treasury in quarterly installments.

All but seven states; Alaska, Florida, Nevada, South Dakota, Texas, Washington and Wyoming; now levy individual state income taxes, administered in a manner similar to federal taxes. In 1939, Philadelphia became the first city to enact an income tax, and although other cities have followed suit, these taxes supply only five percent of municipal tax collections in the nation.

Problems and Controversies

The traditional appeal of the income tax has come from its wide acceptance as an equitable tax, closely related to an individual's ability to pay. For many years, the income tax provided large federal revenues without imposing heavy burdens on the great majority of people.

By the mid-20th century, serious criticisms of tax loopholes and inequities were heard. Concerted attempts at reform resulted only in a more complex and eroded tax base. The situation worsened in the 1970s as surging inflation pushed people into higher tax brackets even though their incomes were barely keeping pace with rising prices. This squeeze further undermined public confidence in the fairness of the income tax. At the same time, it created strong incentives to exploit tax shelters and other loopholes as well as to conceal off-the-record income. Built-in inflation adjustments were adopted, first by a number of states and then in 1985, by the federal government.

Income tax policy is inevitably controversial because it rests essentially on judgment that must be constantly reconsidered as social values change. The complex task of delineating the many deductions and exclusions to be allowed from income because they either make for greater fairness among taxpayers or promote worthy social goals is one of the most difficult and politically sensitive problems faced by government today.

Another major area of controversy is whether wages and salaries should be taxed the same way as business profits or investment income. While some countries and a few states in the United States explicitly apply separate sets of rules to the measurement of different kinds of taxable income, others, like most state's governments, seek to treat all sources of income in the same manner. Even so, dissimilarities inevitably arise. Some costs of earning income are more readily deducted from business and self-employment receipts than they are from wages and salaries. Inflation, by eroding the value of capital, distorts the measurement of income from that source.

Complex adjustments to the tax law could, in principle, eliminate these imbalances. Most countries have preferred simpler, more arbitrary solutions such as taxing capital gains on long-held assets more leniently than other types of income.

European countries typically give corporation shareholders some credit for taxes paid on their profits by corporations. The United States has yet to adopt such relief from the double taxation of dividend income. In 1986, the federal government lowered the corporate tax rate significantly below the levels prevailing in most other developing nations.

This move was part of what was widely called an unprecedented tax reform. Whereas previous tax changes had typically added more deductions and exclusions, thereby further eroding the tax base, the Tax Reform Act of 1986 substantially widened the base, using the prospect of dramatically lower tax rates to persuade people to give up some of their favorite loopholes. Whether this trade-off will long endure remains to be seen, and most likely it will change numerous times in the future.

How steep the progressive tax rate schedule should be is another sensitive issue. Inherent in this problem is the effect of taxes on incentives to work, save, and invest. Although some people work less when they are subjected to high marginal rates, others work more to have more after-tax income. The net effect on the economy has been hard to measure, but there is growing evidence of work disincentives, although the lower rates on personal income of the 1986 act could modify that trend.

Effects on investment decisions are much clearer, ranging from those deliberately stimulated by the tax law to unintentional ones such as the discouragement to investment because of overtaxing inflation-swollen profits and capital gains.

The Tax Reform Act increased the risk that these inflation generated disincentives would reoccur by eliminating the investment tax credit, decelerating depreciation allowances substantially, and taxing capital gains fully on a non-inflation adjusted basis.

Worldwide experience has shown that the income tax can be fairly and efficiently administered only where taxpayer compliance is high. This requires public record keeping and reporting as well as an educated and cooperative population. Where any of these elements are lacking, as in most developing nations, the personal tax tends to fall inequitably on income such as wages that can be easily traced.

Social Security

Social Security is a public program designed to provide income and services to individuals in the event of retirement, sickness, disability, death or unemployment.

In the United States, the term social security refers specifically to the programs established under the Social Security Act, originally enacted in 1935. The original act was a comprehensive law consisting of eleven titles, or subjects, six of which detailed specific programs. The rest established methods of taxation to fund the programs and provided guidelines for the creation of public health facilities. The six original program titles were Old Age Assistance, Old Age Benefits, Unemployment Compensation, aid to Dependent Children, Maternal and Child Welfare, and Aid to the Blind. Benefits for retired adults were the keystone measure of the act and are the portion most often referred to as social security. In 1937, the government began issuing social security cards to all United States citizens to keep track of people's wages and social security taxes, from which benefits would be financed.

Since it's inception in 1935, the Social Security Act has been modified more than twenty times by major amendments. A 1939 amendment to the act added benefit support to retired workers' dependents and to survivors of deceased workers. In the same year, the Social Security Board was made a division of the new cabinet level agency named the Federal Security Agency.

The board was replaced by a newly organized Social Security Administration in 1946. The government reorganized the social security administration in 1949, moving administration of Unemployment Compensation to the United States Department of Labor.

A 1950 amendment to social security added Cost of Living Adjustments to increase benefit payments in order to keep up with inflation. In 1953, the Social Security Agency became a division of another new cabinet agency, the Department of Health, Education, and Welfare. Another major amendment to the act in 1956 added benefits for disabled workers. All of the amendments up to that point in time had created what is now known as the centerpiece of social security, Old Age, Survivors', and Disability Insurance.

A 1965 amendment signed into law by the President Lyndon B. Johnson created Medicare. Medicare is a program that provides hospital insurance to the elderly, along with supplementary medical insurance for other medical costs. In 1972, the original Old Age Assistance and Aid to the Blind titles were combined with new provisions for assistance to disabled people to create a program called Supplemental Security Income.

In 1983, during the administration of the President Ronald W. Reagan, concern for the financial integrity of social security prompted the passage of major legislative changes, including the ending and in some cases, taxation of certain benefits. At this time, the Congress of the United States also legislated a gradual increase in the standard retirement age, raising it from 65 to 67 years of age for individuals born in 1960 or later.

In 1996, President Bill Clinton signed welfare reform bills that were submitted by the United States Congress, which created Temporary Aid for Needy Families as a replacement for Aid to Families with Dependent Children. These bills also made changes to the provision of Social Security Income particularly by denying benefits for most non-citizens.

Temporary Aid for Needy Families is administered by State governments and is supported by the Administration for Children and Families within the United States Department of Health and Human Services. This department took over the health and social welfare components of the Heath, Education, and Welfare division in 1979. The Social Security Administration and the Health Care Financing Administration Department of Health and Human Services administer Medicare. The United States Employment and Training Administration, a division of the Department of Labor, administer Unemployment Compensation.

The taxing provisions for financing Old Age, Survivors' and Disability Insurance along with Unemployment Compensation are part of the Internal Revenue Code. The Internal Revenue Service administers these provisions. Social Security programs are now operated by the independent Social Security Administration, which operated as a division of the Department of Health and Human Services between 1980 and 1995.

The Old Age, Survivors' and Disability Insurance, Medicare Hospital Insurance, and Medicare Supplementary Medical Insurance are separately financed segments of the social security program. The Old Age, Survivors' and Disability Insurance program provides benefits for the aged, for the disabled, and for the survivors of deceased workers.

The cash benefits for the Old Age, Survivors' and Disability Insurance Act are financed by earmarked payroll taxes levied on employees, their employers, and the self-employed. The rate of these contributions is based on the employee's taxable earnings, up to a maximum taxable amount, with the employer contributing an equal amount. Self-employed people contribute twice the amount levied on employees.

The hospital insurance portion of Medicare is, for the most part, similarly financed through payroll taxes. The Supplementary Medical Insurance part of Medicare, which applies to the physicians' services, is financed in part by uniform monthly contributions from aged and disabled persons enrolled in the program and in part by federal general revenues. Legislation was passed in 1982 and 1984 to freeze the share of cost covered by federal revenues at 75%.

The rate of employee contribution, which was 1% when the program began in 1937,is now 7.65%. Of the 7.65%, 6.2% was slated for Old Age, Survivors', and Disability Insurance while 1.45% was for hospital insurance.

In 1996, 124 million people contributed to social security funds during an average month. 43 million people drew social security cash benefits during that same period.

The wages, salaries, and self-employment income of the primary earner or earners should determine the amount of a person's cash benefits in a family. Dependent children and a non-contributing spouse receive additional amounts.

The law specifies certain minimum and maximum monthly benefits. To keep the cash benefits in line with inflation, they are annually indexed to the increase in the cost of living as it is gauged in the consumer price index.

Social Security Benefits replace a stated portion of a person's former earned income, expressed as a percentage of earnings in the year before retirement. Low earners receive a larger percentage of their former income as benefits than recipients from higher income brackets.

An earner's noncontributing spouse, first claiming benefits at age 65 or older, receives 50% of the amount paid to the earner. Similar percentages are payable to disabled individuals and their spouses. Surviving spouses and children receive a percentage of the retirement benefit computed from the earnings of the deceased earner.

The 1986 amendments to the Age Discrimination in Employment Act stated that with some exceptions, an individual could not be compelled to retire because of age. Since 1983, individuals 70 years of age and older were entitled to receive full social security benefits even if they continued to work. For other eligible workers, the amount of benefits is based on age and earnings.

Unemployment Compensation

The United States Unemployment Compensation Program established by the Social Security Act of 1935 and employment service programs established in 1933 form a federal-state cooperative system. The Federal Unemployment Tax Act levied taxes on employers' payrolls to finance unemployment payments. Most of this federal tax can be offset by employer contributions to state funds under an approved state unemployment compensation law. A small portion of the tax is retained by the federal government to pay for the administrative costs of the unemployment compensation and employment service programs, and for loans to states whose fund run low.

State financing and benefit laws vary widely. In general, unemployment compensation benefits under state laws are intended to replace about 50% of an average worker's previous wages. Maximum weekly benefit provisions result in benefits of less than 50% for higher earning workers. All states pay benefits to some unemployed persons for a period of twenty-six weeks. In some states, the duration of benefits depends on the amount earned and the number of weeks worked in a previous year. In other states, all recipients are entitled to benefits for the same length of time. During periods of heavy unemployment, federal law authorizes extended benefits, in some cases up to 39 weeks. In 1975, extended benefits were payable for up to 65 weeks. Extended benefits are financed in part by federal employer taxes.

Supplemental Security Income and Other Programs

Under the Supplemental Security Income Program, the federal government provides payments to needy, aged, blind, and disabled individuals. These programs were cut back during the early 1980s and again in the late 1990s. Both general budgetary constraints and anti-welfare sentiments motivated cutbacks.

In determining the amount of aid given, programs take into consideration the income and resources of individuals and families. Under the Social Security Act, the federal government also provides to the states financial grants for maternal and child health, disabled children's services, child welfare services and social services such as day care for children of working mothers.

In 1995, Old Age, Survivors', and Disability Insurance benefits, the largest of all social insurance payments, amounted to 4.5% of the gross domestic product. In the future, the percentage of Gross Domestic Product, used to support income-maintenance and health programs, will likely increase. This will happen due to such factors as the growing number of senior citizens in the United States, an overall increasing population, expanding investment in private pension and health plans, and the rising cost of medical care.

Now that you have a basic knowledge of income taxation, we can go through your income and the taxation of it. In this section we will also show you the basics about filing your income tax return.

The W-4 Form

Before you begin working for a new employer, you should complete form W-4. The W-4 form is the Employee Withholding Allowance Certificate. This is the basis for determining how much money your employer will take out of each of your paychecks for contribution towards your income taxes. Each paycheck that you receive will have taxes withheld from it to pay Federal and State taxes, Unemployment and State Disability Income taxes, Social Security tax contributions, and Medicare tax contributions. We have discussed all of these forms of income tax earlier in this section.

On the W-4 form, you will complete your basic information, which includes your name, address, city, state, and zip code. You will also include your social security number and declare your marital status. You will need to determine what exemptions you are declaring. The

W-4 form gives you a worksheet to calculate your exemptions. For each exemption declared, fewer taxes are withheld from your check. This gives you more spendable income as you earn it, however, if you are not careful you will owe additional income tax when you file your return at the end of the year. The idea to consider when deciding how much to have withheld from your paycheck, is to get as close to what you estimate your income tax to be. That way, you will not have more deducted from your check than you need nor will you be in a position of having to pay the Internal Revenue Service additional tax money at the end of your tax year. You can review the Personal Allowance Worksheet, Deductions and Adjustments Worksheet, Two-Earner/Two-Job Worksheet, and the Employee's Withholding Allowance Certificate. You should evaluate your withholdings annually to make certain they are still applicable to your personal situation.

Filing Your Income Tax Return

After the end of the year, usually sometime during the month of January, your employer will provide you with the W-2 Form. The W-2 form is the Wage and Tax Statement. This is basically a statement of how much gross earnings you received during the prior year along with the amounts of taxes withheld by your employer and paid on your behalf towards your income tax due for that period. The figures on the W-2 form are annualized figures. You will need the W-2 form in order to prepare your income tax return to be filed with the Internal Revenue Service each year. If you worked for more than one employer during the year, each employer will need to provide you with a separate W-2 form.

If you are paid as an Independent Contractor, as salespersons or laborers often are, the employer does not withhold any taxes on your behalf. This means that you will receive your gross income up front without making tax contributions as you earn the money. In cases such as this, the employer will provide you with a 1099 Form. The 1099 Form states Miscellaneous Income. It will show the gross amount you receive from the employer. If you don't receive a 1099 Form from your employee that does not relieve you of your responsibility to report this income to the Internal Revenue Service and pay the appropriate taxes due. Failure to report income to the Internal Revenue Service could result in extreme penalties.

Income Tax Forms for Federal Tax Filing

For most people who are just getting started, the 1040 EZ form or the 1040 Form are used for filing income taxes. Individuals or persons filing joint returns with dependents use the 1040 Form. For those individuals or persons filing jointly with no dependents, the 1040EZ Form can be used.. Completing the return is really fairly simple. Each line number has instructions about what needs to be entered and tells you what to do as a next step. The form must be signed and your W-2 form(s) attached prior to mailing it to the Internal Revenue Service. The form normally specifies the date by which the return must be date stamped by the United States Postal Service. Typically, it is April 15th. However, if the 15th falls on a Sunday, there may be a variation to this. If your return is not mailed by the due date, the Internal Revenue Service will assess a fee for the late filing and if additional tax monies are due with the filing, they will assess interest to that amount. Always file your taxes in plenty of time for them to be considered on time!

State Income Tax Forms

Depending on the State that you reside in, a State Income Tax return will be filed each year along with the Federal Income Tax Return. Check with your local Franchise Tax Board for the appropriate forms to use with your State Income Tax filing if applicable.

We cannot stress the importance of understanding your tax situation and filing and paying taxes appropriately. There are grave consequences for not complying with Internal Revenue laws. For that reason, it might be prudent to seek the advice of a licensed tax consultant when preparing your tax return. If you have someone such as a Certified Public Accountant or a Tax Service prepare your income tax return on your behalf, that person will need to sign the return in addition to you. However, you should be aware that you are ultimately responsible for accurate tax payment and filing requirements with the Internal Revenue Service.

Chapter Thirteen Summary

1. The history of income tax

- Originally, the United States constitution prohibited the federal government from levying direct taxes, except in proportion to population

- Constitutional amendment was required to give full, legal sanction to federal use of an income tax

- In 1913, the ratification of the 16th amendment to the constitution allowed the taxing of income

2. Your personal income tax responsibilities

- You as an individual, are required to file an income tax return with the Internal Revenue Service (IRS) on your gross income

- Your personal income tax returns are due on (or before) April 15.

- During the year, an employer must withhold the taxes due on the wages of the employees, and pay such taxes to the United States Treasury

3. Problems and Controversies

- In the beginning, income tax provided large federal revenues without imposing heavy burdens on the great majority of people

- By mid-century, serious criticisms of tax loopholes and inequities were heard

- By the mid-1980's inflation adjustments were adopted by the government

- Income tax is highly controversial because it rests on judgments that must be constantly reconsidered as social values change

4. Social Security

- Is a program designed to provide income and services to individuals in the event of retirement, sickness, disability, death, or unemployment

- The Social Security Act was originally enacted in 1935

- Social Security Cards began being issued in 1937, to keep track of people's wages and Social Security taxes

- In 1965, an amendment signed into law by Lyndon B. Johnson created Medicare

- In 1983, President Reagan, concerned about financial integrity, enacted many changes in the Social Security system

- In 1996, President Clinton signed welfare reform bills that created "temporary aid for needy families" as a replacement for "Aid to families with dependent children

5. Some Basic Tax Forms are

- The W-4 Form – Employee Withholding

- The W-2 Form – Wage and Tax Statement that the employer provides

- 1099 Form – for miscellaneous income

- 1040 EZ Form – Federal income tax filing form for individuals or persons filing jointly

Chapter Thirteen Quiz

1. What is the sixteenth (16th) amendment?

2. What are you stating on a federal income tax return? Be specific.

3. Describe the controversial side of income taxes.

4. When was Social Security founded and what is it?

5. List the four basic tax form and describe when each is used.

CHAPTER FOURTEEN
RECORDKEEPING

Recordkeeping And Planning

Monitoring Your Daily Activities

Measuring Your Progress

Use Of A Daily Planner

Recordkeeping and Why It's Important

It is important to set reasonable goals for yourself, and to evaluate your progress in meeting those goals from time to time. It sometimes becomes necessary to make adjustments to your goals based on life itself.

We have discussed the necessity for balance in your life in earlier sections. At times, it may seem that your life is out of control or seemingly, you may perceive that you are not heading in the direction you had intended for yourself. At times like this, it is best to be able to sit down and take a look at what your goals and priorities are. You may elect to make some modifications in order for you to re-establish balance in your life

Planning requires you to get in touch with your dreams and connect them with the reality of your world. Everything begins with a thought or a dream. Motivation puts those thoughts and dreams into motion.

Tracking Your Activities

One very important habit to get into is tracking your daily activities. By doing this, you are able to realize your accomplishments, evaluate your progress, and identify any pattern, that may be resulting in lack of progress. As you go through life, it may seem that some goals are endless journeys with little or no progress being made. If you take a look back at where you established the goal and began putting it in motion, you can more easily recognize your progress, and understand how you may have arrived where you are today.

A very useful tool to use in monitoring your daily activities, along with short and long term goals, is some form of a daily planner. There are many different companies that make planners. With your busier and more hectic lifestyle, a planner is really an essential tool. Not only is it a place to record any important information about your activities as we discussed earlier, but it is also a wonderful way to keep track of daily activities, both from a personal and from a business perspective. It allows you to easily monitor your budget goals. It is a centralized place to keep important names, addresses, telephone numbers, and important dates to remember. It serves as a written method of prioritizing goals and tracking accomplishments. It is a way to become extremely organized.

Tools for Organizing Your Records

Today, planners or organizers come in many forms. There are actual books, hand held computer type planners, and software programs that interface with the hand held version of the planner. With these types of tools, there is no reason why you can't accomplish what you set out to do. One of the best investments you can make in your future is to get into the habit of keeping good records, setting and monitoring your goals, and utilizing some type of organizer planner system to keep track of all of it.

Chapter Fourteen Summary

1. Recordkeeping and Planning

    • It is important to set goals for yourself

    • It may be necessary to make adjustment to your goals based on life itself

2. Monitoring your Daily Activities

    • It's very important to keep track of your daily activities

    • Monitoring your activities helps you evaluate your progress or lack of progress

3. Measuring your Progress

    • Keeping a daily planner helps you to monitor your budget as well as your activities and your progress in meeting your goals

Chapter Fourteen Quiz

1. Why is it important to keep good records? Explain your answer.

2. What purpose does monitoring your daily activities serve?

3. Does monitoring your progress help you monitor your budgeting processes? Explain your answer.

CHAPTER FIFTEEN
CONCLUSION

What Was Needed To Survive 200 Years Ago

Survival Skills For The 21st Century

What Everyone Expects You To Know.....

And At Last, You Do........

Life 200 Years Ago

Two hundred years ago, the skills required in order to be able to survive on your own were entirely different than what is required in today's world. Let's think about what might have been important in order to survive two hundred years ago. The following list might offer a few ideas:

- Ownership of a rifle and the knowledge and skill to use it

- Knowledge of how to hunt and kill wild game in order to eat

- Knowledge of how to make your own furniture and clothing from rustic materials

- The ability to grow your own food for canning in preparation for winter

- Tools and physical ability to cut and split wood to keep warm during the winter

- Basic knowledge of how to handle basic and more complicated medical emergencies

- Ownership of a horse to travel with

- Knowledge of what foods growing in the wild are edible and what is deadly

- The ability to protect yourself from the enemy, animals, and the natural elements

Two hundred years ago we didn't have any modern conveniences. Life was rustic and raw. Only the hardy were to survive. In fact, the average life expectancy was really quite short due to the physical hardships, diseases that had no cures, etc. Two hundred years ago, stress was more than likely defined very differently than it is today. Our forefathers endured the challenges of their time and made progress that ultimately resulted in our modern world. Two hundred years ago, young people were sent into the world as adults at an earlier age than we are today.

Those young people were probably better prepared for what their life skills needed to be than are many young people today.

Life Today

Today, our society operates in a completely different manner than it did two hundred years ago. Things are much faster paced. We enjoy many modern conveniences. Our survival skills are much more intellectually geared than they are physically geared. We live in a complex system which is rapidly changing all the time. During the last century we have seen many modifications made in the areas of technology, housing, and social services, and those changes have resulted in many current issues which must be addressed. One thing is certain; nothing stays the same for long. We must be on our toes and adaptive to the many changes which occur and have a direct effect on our lives. We must be informed and educated and we must have certain skills adaptive to our modern world if we are going to survive and be successful in our lifetime.

Let's Summarize What We Have Learned

Let's list a few of the skills that we have outlined in this book. We believe these skills are essential to you becoming a self-sufficient, successful individual:

- Knowledge of how to make a good solid decision for yourself

- Knowledge of how to secure income in order to survive financially, including establishing a resume, interviewing for the job and securing the job

- Understanding the concept of transportation and meeting your own need for transportation

- Housing essentials, including getting your own place to live in

- Understanding the basic concept of the exchange of money today including the establishment of basic banking needs and how to manage them

- The ability to budget money, including how to prioritize your wants and needs

- Knowledge of how to establish, maintain, and build credit including the advantages and disadvantages of operating in the world of credit

- Communicating your personal data as regards to your health

- Understanding and exercising your right to vote and serve as a juror

- Managing all the financial responsibilities and still having quality in your life

- Owning your own home

- Understanding the advantages of serving in one of the branches of the Armed Forces

- Understanding income taxation

- Understanding our Social Security System in order to be prepared for your senior years

- Understanding the need and knowing how to set goals and monitor your progress in meeting those goals in order to progress in your life including managing your time which is probably the most valuable asset in today's busy world!

As you can see, the survival skills needed for today's world are altogether different than those needed two hundred years ago. We really don't need to know how to kill wild game in order to eat, but we do need to have the money in order to go to the market and buy the food we need to survive.

It has been our goal to fill in the gap between what our traditional system of education teaches and what we have found to be needed in our own lives, and then to provide that knowledge to people who are just starting out on that wonderful journey called life. Our hope is that this information will enable you to be successful and fulfilled during your lifetime, while living in this ever changing, challenging, highly technical world we call our own. Thank you for letting us share our experiences with you. YOU CAN DO IT, WE KNOW YOU CAN!

André J. Olivan, Author and Designer

Amber G. Olivan, Author and Managing Editor

Chapter Fifteen Summary

1. What was needed 200 years ago:

- There were no modern conveniences 200 years ago

- Life was rustic and raw

- Life expectancy was quite short

2. What we have today:

- Pace is much faster

- Our survival skills are much more intellectually geared

- Stress is much higher in today's lifestyle

3. We think you can, we know you can!

- Thank you for letting us share our experiences with you. Just remember, you have an entire lifetime to learn and grow!